DA COACH

DA COACH

Rich Wolfe

TRIUMPH
B O O K S
CHICAGO

This book is available in quantity at special discounts for your group or organization. For more information, contact:

Triumph Books
601 South LaSalle Street
Chicago, Illinois 60605
(312) 939-3330 FAX (312) 663-3557

Book design by Patricia Frey
Cover design by Mike Mulligan

Rights/Permissions: Rich Wolfe

Every effort to secure permission to reproduce copyrighted material has been made. Apologies are made for any errors or omissions.

Front cover photo: Heinz Kluetmeier/Sports Illustrated
Back cover photo: Greg Heisler/ESPN the Magazine

Printed in the United States of America

ISBN 1-57243-439-2

Table of Contents

Acknowledgements

A project like this would not have been possible without the help of good friends like Jon Spoelstra, Dale Ratermann, John Counsell, Jim Murray, Gene Cervelli, Cappy Gagnon, and Jim Wisniewski; real professionals like Russ Russell at *The Dallas Cowboys Weekly*, Paul Jensen of the Arizona Cardinals, Ken Valdiserri of the Chicago Bears, Ed Rose of the *Beaver County Times*, Ben Manges of the University of Pittsburgh Athletic Department, Jim Prokell, and Beano Cook; and especially the wonderful people like Kathy and Steve Moffit at Petty Motorsports in Greensboro, NC, and Ann Verhulst at Old World Industries in Northbrook, IL. Thanks should also go to Peter Bannon at Sports Publishing Inc., and Ernie Roth and John Nolan at Contemporary Books; previous Ditka book authors Don Pierson and Armen Keyteyian for their kind offers of help; and outstanding writers like Gregg Lewis, Bob Verdi, Pat Smith, John Tullius, and Bob Greene.

But the biggest thanks go to prolific author Peter Golenbock, for his research notes; Richard Whittingham, the author of many books, including the four best-written books about the Chicago Bears; and Ellen Brewer, the smartest, most beautiful woman in the whole state of Oklahoma and the Sooner State's best typist since a senior at Henryetta (OK) High School named Troy Aikman won the Oklahoma State Boys' Typing Championship in 1984.

To Gene Cervelli and Jon Spoelstra,
good friends and great guys.

To Special K, who is great in every way.

Introduction

Why a book on Ditka? Because Ditka is a character at a time when the world is running out of characters. Orthodox behavior has totally stifled creativity. Posturing and positioning one's image in order to maximize income has replaced honesty and bluntness. Political correctness has made phonies out of too many. But not Ditka—when he said New Orleans was filthy, he was right. In 1997, when he said Doug Flutie could play in the NFL and that he wanted to sign him for the Saints, he was right, even though the critics laughed at him.

Recently I did a book on Harry Caray—a character if ever there was one. One of the people I interviewed for Harry's book was Mike Ditka, a guy I've always liked. He was a great interview, very generous with his time, and really interesting. We talked about Harry Caray for five minutes, about football for five minutes, and about life in general for almost an hour. Most impressive was his conversation about his personal spiritual evolution and the effect it's had on his life.

So doing a book on Ditka seemed a natural progression. He was a character. I liked him, it would be fun, and you just knew there would be a lot of good stories. And what an experience it's been. The gentleness in the voices of fierce competitors like Jerry West and Gale Sayers was surprising. Beano Cook was a riot. The sincerity and drive of Coach Dave McGinnis made me realize the Bears made a bad mistake in not hiring him. The Varmint brothers deserve an entire book of their own. The Kyle Petty people were the most professional, and in a really nice way. Ditka was blunt, which was fine, and wary, which is understandable. Hall of Famer Jack Ham was nicely businesslike, humble, and quick-witted, but the athletic department at his alma mater, Penn State, was exactly the opposite.

The world was different when I was young. For one thing, it was flat, according to my sons. Notre Dame University is 307 miles from my hometown of Lost Nation, Iowa, and Lost Nation, Iowa, is about a million miles from Notre Dame. So it was with more than a little trepidation that I left the farm in the early sixties and headed to South Bend on a baseball scholarship. But I thought, "How tough could it be?" In Iowa, there were four colleges bigger than Notre Dame. I quickly found out that Notre Dame was another planet athletically. Fifty-one of my schoolmates would be drafted by the NFL or the AFL. My roommate would later play for the New York Mets. Four pitchers on the baseball team would also make the major leagues and one of them would play several years in the NBA. A Heisman trophy winner lived in the dormitory adjacent to mine. Because of alphabetical seating, I sat next to Carl Yastrzemski in a couple of fall classes. The sons of Stan Musial, Eddie Arcaro, and Don Dunphy were also students at that time. Don Criqui was a student-station sports announcer. A freshman basketball teammate of mine was Jon Spoelstra, who later became president and/or general manager of three NBA teams. And Don Ohlmeyer, who started Monday Night Football and also inaugurated the Skins Game in golf, was a classmate.

For a sports fan like me it was an exhilarating experience. But the one athlete who really stood out to this wide-eyed freshman was an end from Pitt named Mike Ditka. Better on defense than offense, the meanest, strongest, and toughest athlete I had ever seen, before or since—guys like Ditka simply didn't exist where I came from.

I know what you're thinking: Didn't this gifted writer just end a sentence with a preposition? Yep. 'Cause that's just how most people talk, including me. This is a book written by a sports fan for other sports fans—not for publishers, not for editors, not for critics.

It's not to say we don't take criticism well. If you have any, just jot them down on the back of a twenty-dollar bill and send them to my attention in care of the publisher.

This book is mainly about Mike Ditka, but there will be a fair amount of meandering into areas that seemed too interesting not to include. We'll eavesdrop and find out some fascinating tidbits about Ann-Margret, the Chicago Cubs, Leon Spinks, and the Dallas Cowboys, among others.

The best thing about athletes, particularly the older ones, is that they tell great stories. The best thing about writing a book is meeting these people, getting to know them, and sharing the laughter. As you will see, some remember the same events differently, but all of them rejoice in the memories.

Enjoy your reading, 'cause this book could turn you into "park bench" material.

> Rich Wolfe
> October, 1999
> Pittsburgh, Pennsylvania

Chapter 1

photo courtesy of *Dallas Cowboys Weekly*

Ken Clapper

Joseph Haller

Jerry West

Foge Fazio

Don Hennon

Paul Martha

Beano Cook

George Kiseda

Maury Youmans

College Days

STEALING DITKA
KEN CLAPPER

*As an undergraduate at Pitt, Ken Clapper never went to a single
Pitt football game. Yet he was the key to recruiting Pitt's legendary Mike Ditka. Clapper has had a very successful career in
the insurance business in Altoona, which is about two hours east
of Pittsburgh.*

A few years ago, I was chairman of the cancer drive in Blair
County, Pennsylvania. Seated beside me at the kickoff
luncheon was Joe Paterno. I told Joe the story about how
I stole Ditka from Penn State, and he could hardly eat his lunch.

It was the summer of 1957 and I got a call from Pitt's coach. We
were good friends. John said, "Are you having some baseball thing
over there next week?" I said, "Yeah, we're having the national ama-
teur baseball federation." He said, "There was a left fielder on the
Pittsburgh team. He's a good football player. He's going to Penn
State. But at least touch base with him. His name's Mike Ditka."

So the Pittsburgh team came in and they stayed at a real cruddy
hotel—it was just the luck of the draw. I tracked him down. I said,
"Mike, would you like to go to dinner?" I took him to dinner, we had
a nice chat, but I didn't really make any progress. So I followed the
Pittsburgh team the next day and that night I again asked, "Mike, want
to go to dinner?" I don't know what made me say it. At dinner I asked
Mike, "What do you think you want to do in life?" "Oh," he said, "I
think I want to be a dentist, maybe even an oral surgeon." I said, "Well,
we just had a new oral surgery clinic open up here recently. Would you
like to see it?" He said, "Yeah, I'd like to see it." He was nice. He was-
n't a smarty like he is now.

Joe Paterno

So I talked to the manager of the Pittsburgh team. I said, "Could we take Ditka through the oral surgery clinic?" He said, "Yeah, on the way out of town." They were eliminated on Thursday, and they stopped by on the way out of town.

I got the oral surgeon, Joe Haller, off the golf course. He didn't even change his shoes—he was still wearing his golf shoes. The team parked outside the clinic. We took Ditka in and talked to him about dentistry, oral surgery, and things of this type.

Meanwhile, the team was waiting outside for Ditka. We were ready to close the thing down, and Ditka looked at me and said, "Mr. Clapper, do you think Mr. Engle would be mad if I changed my mind and decided to go to Pitt?" I said, "Oh no, Mike. Mr. Engle is interested in your education as well as your football." He said, "Well, I think that's what I'll do." He went outside, got in the car, and started back home. I called John and said, "John, get your ass down to Aliquippa with your feet under the kitchen table. We've got Ditka." He said, "You've got to be kidding; he's committed to Penn State." I said, "Just do what I tell you." John drove to Aliquippa and Ditka said, "Yeah, I want to go to Pitt."

They took Ditka, a high school fullback by the name of J. M. Cunningham, and another player to Pitt, and they registered them

Q: Red Grange was nicknamed "Old Seventy-Seven," "The Wheaton Iceman," and "The Galloping Ghost." What was his fourth nickname?
A: Red. His first name was Harold.

for classes. Then they took them to Lake Erie and hid them for three days. After school had started, they brought them down and put them in classes.

In the meantime, Paterno, who was an assistant at Penn at the time, was over at the Pitt campus, saying, "I know you've got Ditka here some-where." He never found Ditka until after Ditka was in class. That is how Ditka got to Pitt. He came to Altoona intending to go to Penn State, and left here going to Pitt.

> **"I think I want to be a dentist, maybe even an oral surgeon."**

I don't know how he did in that baseball tournament. But he was a good baseball player. And he's liable to hit you for writing this book.

DR. MIKE DITKA
JOSEPH HALLER

Joseph Haller is a retired oral surgeon from Altoona, Pennsylvania, now living in Vero Beach, Florida. It was in his clinic that Ditka decided to become a dentist and enroll in the University of Pittsburgh, thus forsaking Joe Paterno and the Nittany Lions.

We had a guy who really promoted Pitt like crazy—Kenny Clapper. I had never heard of Mike Ditka before Kenny Clapper got a hold of me and wanted me to meet him. Ditka was in Altoona playing in a baseball tournament. Kenny wanted Ditka to meet me because he wanted Ditka to go to dental school at Pitt. One of the reasons Ditka went to Pitt was because he had a chance to get into one of the professional schools—either medicine or dentistry. Those other schools like Penn State didn't have a dental school.

They took me off the golf course to meet him. I walked into my clinic with my golf shoes on. I'm a neural and oral facial surgeon. I do all the facial stuff—give people new chins, new jaws, etc. They wanted him to see that. I worked him over a little bit and finally he decided to go. I'll tell you one thing—he wanted to be a doctor.

We told Ditka that if he was a good enough student to get into Pitt, he probably could get into dental school, because the coach at Pitt used to get a lot of guys into dental school.

The other players were sitting out front in their cars, waiting for him. He was still in his baseball uniform. I was in my golfing outfit. My office and golf course were only ten minutes from where they were playing baseball. He was at the clinic for about an hour or an hour and a half. The only other person

He wanted to be a doctor . . . He made out better; he ended up a coach.

with him was Kenny Clapper from Altoona. Kenny was a big supporter of Pitt for many years, and he wanted Ditka to go to Pitt. He was actually more responsible for Ditka going to Pitt than I was. He wanted me to add some muscle to it. I knew everybody over at Pitt, and Kenny knew I could get Ditka into the dental school since the dean was a good friend of mine. I was a trustee and I was also on the state dental board.

My first impression of Ditka was that he was a big, strong kid. They told me that he was a good football player and a good baseball player. I was impressed with the guy, and he seemed pretty sincere. He expressed himself very well. I said, "Are you sure you want to go to dental school?" He said, "Yes, that's what I want to be." Of course, he never got that far. He made out better; he ended up a coach.

I've seen Ditka quite a few times since then. Three years ago, I played in a tournament in California for Frank Sinatra before he died. Ditka always played in those tournaments, and I had a chance to talk to him a little bit. He didn't remember me.

> Mike Ditka is the only man to score a Super Bowl touchdown and coach a Super Bowl winner.

photo courtesy of L.A. Lakers

DEATH WISH
JERRY WEST

Jerry West, such an NBA legend that he was the model for the NBA logo, was arguably the best defensive guard ever. He is the only MVP of an NBA Finals who played for the losing team. His long and successful career as a Hall of Fame player, coach, and general manager began in his hometown of Cabin Creek, West Virginia, and continued on to the courts of West Virginia University.

The University of Pittsburgh was our biggest and most bitter rival because the two schools were only about ninety minutes apart. We would win the games at our court in Morgantown fairly easily. We would never be threatened as much as when we played at Pitt. The games at Pitt were really hard-fought, close games, very competitive and very physical.

In 1958, during my junior year, we played a game at Pitt. It was a field house-like place, and around their court they had a running track. At one end of the court, there was no seating, just a curtain and, behind that, the running track.

Q: What was the previous name of the Big Ten Conference?
A: It was called the Big Nine after the University of Chicago dropped out following the 1939 season. It became the Big Ten again when Michigan State joined in the early 1950s.

Of course, I had no idea who Mike Ditka was, but I met him that night. Early in the game, I faked out my defender and was driving for an easy layup. Ditka absolutely creamed me and deposited me over this curtain that kept dust off the floor. While I was scraping cinders off my arms and legs, one of my teammates said something to him. Ditka called him a "snake," but to use the language, called him a particular kind of snake, and said he would break his neck. All throughout the game, you knew Mike was around. He was just an aggressive player.

Was Ditka a good player?

"Oh, Mike was a great football player."

No, I mean, was Ditka a good basketball player?

"Like I told you, Mike was an excellent football player."

MEMORIES OF "THE HAMMER"
FOGE FAZIO

Foge Fazio is the assistant coach for the Minnesota Vikings and a former Pitt head coach. The Coriapolis, Pennsylvania, native has played with and against Ditka since childhood.

Mike went to a larger high school than I did, but I knew him then and watched him play. He was a year behind me at the University, and we were on teams together. We also played American Legion baseball against each other.

During his sophomore year he went out for the basketball team at Pitt and made the team. We were playing at West Virginia, and they put him in the game. Jerry West and all those guys just got the hell out of the way. His nickname was "the Hammer." Naturally, Mike was the hammer and the enforcer, but he also liked to shoot the ball. He would take a couple of shots now and then, and we would be sitting in the stands going crazy cheering for him.

Mike is such a competitor. He was playing shortstop in one of our games, and someone hit a ball out to center field, where his brother Ashton was playing. Ashton came in and got the ball, but he didn't throw it to the cut-off guy. Mike was so pissed he threw his hat down and went after Ashton. Ashton saw him coming, took off running, and went over a chain-link fence to get out of his way. The game was delayed until Mike got back, and then they had to put in a new center fielder. I don't think Mike caught up with Ashton, but I'm sure he got him later at home. Mike was a good shortstop. He had great range and was a good hitter and leader, just like he was in football.

We were playing Boston College at Boston College my senior year. In those days, when we scored a touchdown we had to line up and kick off. So basically we were on the kickoff cover team, too. If you started on defense and offense, you had to cover the kickoffs.

> **I'm sure he was bruised as hell, but you never would have known it.**

It was a pretty tough game and we had just pulled ahead of them. Mike was all fired up, running up and down the line, smacking guys on their helmets. He smacked one guard, Norton, and almost knocked him down. I saw him coming and ducked. Then he went up to Jimbo Cunningham, who was a big, tough fullback. He smacked Jimbo on the head and they almost got into a fistfight. People had to separate them right there before the kickoff.

One week we were getting ready to play Syracuse, the national champions. On the Thursday before the game, we were at our place doing a practice session without pads. They threw a long pass to Mike and he went down the field and caught it. Just as he caught it, he ran smack into the blocking sled, which was a two-man steel sled without the pads. A hush fell over the whole place. He just jumped right up. He had a big gash on his hand, and I'm sure he was bruised as hell, but you never would have known it. He still came out and played that Saturday. Most people would have been lying in the hospital. He is just a tough, tough individual.

> **Mike would somehow go off his block and just knock the hell out of the ball carrier. He was a crusher.**

We played a 5–3 defense. I played outside linebacker either beside Mike or just behind him. I'd go to make a tackle, and all at once I would hear a "boom"—Mike would somehow go off his block and just knock the hell out of the ball carrier, before I could get there. I was shocked when he went to the NFL and played tight end. I thought for sure he would be a linebacker or a defensive end. He was a crusher. He was an outstanding defensive man.

I went to the Patriots in 1960. I was cut and went back to see Pitt play Michigan State at Pitt Stadium.

Pitt had to play at 10:00 in the morning so they could get their game out of the way. A big fight broke out between Herb Adderley and Mike Ditka on the field. They probably would still be fighting today, like two gladiators on the field, but some people broke it up. It was one of those rambunctious deals that was momentous at the time.

When I got the head coaching job at Pitt, Mike called and said, "The Italian kid from Coriapolis who went to Pitt and the Slovac kid from Aliquippa who went to Pitt now become head coaches on the same day." He even put that in his book.

We played Illinois one year when the NFL was on strike. Mike came down to the game and gave my players a pep talk and really fired them up. They all knew who Mike was.

He is such a loyal guy. Every year he holds a golf tournament for his high school in Aliquippa. At one time, with the factory, they were probably graduating four or five hundred kids; now, they are graduating about one hundred. He holds the golf tournament to raise money not only for the football program, but for scholarships for needy kids. One year he had just had one of his hips replaced. Another year he played after a knee operation. He is very loyal to his hometown, and he always has been.

We played in an alumni game in the spring of 1977. I was the linebacker coach for Jackie Sherrill at the time and we all played in the game. Mike was coaching the Dallas Cowboys at the time and he came back and played defense. We were thirty-seven years old. But that's the kind of guy he is. He gives back to the people in his hometown.

Q: Who is the only college football player to be MVP of four bowl games?

A: Bo knows it's Bo Jackson, Auburn '82, '83, '84, '85. Marvin Graves of Syracuse came close, winning every year but his senior year. Bo is the only NFL back to have earned two touchdown runs of over ninety yards from a scrimmage.

EXTRA-LARGE PANTIES FOR TWO ALL-AMERICANS
DON HENNON

Although he is only 5'9", Don Hennon became the first All-American basketball player in University of Pittsburgh history. He was Mike Ditka's friend and fraternity brother, and is now a successful surgeon in the Pittsburgh area.

Mike was a good basketball player; he was a very coordinated and talented athlete. He not only played basketball, he also played football and baseball and was a wrestling champ for the interfraternity council. He was an all-around athlete and a real good guy.

He was a junior, one year behind me. When they were initiating us into the fraternity, they had us run around in the basement of the fraternity house in women's panties. We were running around in the basement, and one of the brothers took some ice cubes, pulled Mike's pants back, and dumped the ice down his panties. Mike didn't say anything, but I saw him walk over to a table where there were about a half dozen eggs in a container. He picked the eggs up, went over to the guy—who was wearing a brand new suit—and smashed them over his head. Eggs were running all over him. I thought, "Oh, my goodness, we're going to get thrown out of here for sure." But they didn't throw us out; they went ahead and let us join. What a sight: this guy was all dressed up and thought he was doing something, and BOOM! Eggs all over him.

TAKING CARE OF BUSINESS
PAUL MARTHA

Paul Martha attended Pitt with Mike Ditka, and later went on to enjoy a professional career with the Pittsburgh Steelers and the Denver Broncos.

photo courtesy of the University of Pittsburgh

When I was recruited by Pitt, Mike and I worked a construction job together. He kind of took care of me. We were building a Kaufmann's department store in Monroeville. No one ever fooled around with Michael; therefore, no one ever fooled around with me. Construction is construction and it can get a little physical, but no one ever got physical with Michael.

Michael was a very physical guy, but I never saw him get in a fight. No one really wanted to fight him because he was bigger than most people. He was just Mike Ditka, and people didn't fool around with Mike Ditka.

I think he was a junior then, and I was about to become a freshman. I never really played with Mike, but I played against him when he was with the Bears and I was with the Steelers. In college, we scrimmaged, but we never played on the same team because freshmen weren't eligible in those days.

He was just Mike Ditka, and people didn't fool around with Mike Ditka.

I did play some basketball games with him. I played for Pitt for two years, and we would scrimmage the varsity. Michael wasn't a player with a lot of finesse; he was a big guy and very physical. West Virginia had a good team—Jerry West, Clint Kishbaugh—but we were a little more physical than they were.

He was a pretty good baseball player. He played center field. We both played for the Lawrenceville Tigers, a sandlot team, in Pittsburgh. It was good baseball. A lot of minor league players came back and played.

One season Pitt played USC, and the McKeevers twins, who starred for Southern Cal, gave Ditka a tough time. They picked on him, and the crowd (this part of Pittsburgh was a tough crowd) got on Michael about the McKeevers. The crowd was more Pittsburgh fans than Pitt fans, so they got on Michael. He wasn't doing too well—he had struck out once and had dropped a fly ball—so they got on him. He was out in center field, and I played shortstop. Right in the middle of the inning, he started in from center field, and I said, "Michael, where are you going?" He said, "I've got to take care of business." He just cleaned out the stands; they saw him coming and they just left. Bingo, everybody was immediately gone. Then he came back to center field.

He could have played professional baseball. But in those days, it wasn't worth the effort because they sent you down to the Mexican League. It was a lot easier to play college football.

The rings for the Super Bowl winners cost twice as much as the rings for the losers.

ACHILLES
BEANO COOK

Beano Cook is ESPN's resident college football expert. He still resides in his native Pittsburgh and has known Ditka for a long time.

photo courtesy of ESPN/Rick LaBrache

I first heard about Ditka when he was still a junior in high school. He was a pretty good player; they won a league championship. I heard about him then, but I really started to hear about him in the fall of 1956. The two football players I heard about a lot were Myron Pottios, who ended up captain at Notre Dame, and Mike Ditka, who ended up captain at Pitt.

Everybody wanted Ditka. He was supposed to go to Penn State, but for some reason he changed his mind around August 5 and went to Pitt. Joe Paterno was recruiting for Penn State's head coach Rip Engle, and he had Ditka all set for Penn State. Paterno still says it was his toughest recruiting loss.

Ditka came to Pitt to study dentistry. Can't you see Ditka doing somebody's teeth? Picture Mike putting the novocaine in: "What do you mean, novocaine? Why do you want novocaine? You've got to be a man. Here's the drill." I can just see him opening somebody's mouth and sticking those goddamn things in.

Freshmen couldn't play in those days but the varsity players talked about him. Every so often they scrimmaged and someone would say, "Ditka's some player; he's a rock." When you saw him for the first time, you just had the feeling that this guy was special. I've been wrong before, I guess, but I was right about him; I knew he was special right away, and he was.

Bob Anderson, who played for Army in 1958, Ditka's sophomore year, was a great All-American. He tells a story about the Pitt-Army game in 1958 that cost Army the national title. It was 14–14. Pitt brought the third team ends in, and this guy just about killed Anderson. He found out later that the guy was Mike Ditka.

This was 1958. Nobody knew who the players were. You knew the players in your conference, the Notre Dame quarterback, and that's it. Now they know all their names because of publicity. Later, Anderson said, "You know, I just never got hit like that." He wasn't expecting that from a substitute end.

On the last play of the game against Army, Pitt threw a long pass that was intercepted. Ditka came back to help make the tackle, and he was injured. As he was being carried off the field, an Army player came up to him and said, "You, Mike Ditka, are the greatest football player I've ever seen." He had his arms around the trainer and another player. The trainer told me that story. Mike would not have told me that; he was modest. He wanted to win, but he didn't care about personal glory. He just wanted to win.

The first game Ditka ever started was against Notre Dame at Pittsburgh in 1958. The day before the game, Terry Brennan, Notre Dame's coach, said, "All I know is if I had Mike Ditka, I would start him." The score was 29–26 Pitt. Ditka caught a fourth down pass

> In the 1970s, a St. Louis football Cardinals fan bought an ad in the *St. Louis Post-Dispatch* offering to sell the "Official Cardinals' Playbook" with "all five plays illustrated, including the squib punt."

that kept the drive alive in the last two minutes, and Pitt scored with eleven seconds to go. That's the game that cost Terry Brennan his job, or so they say.

In those days, Ditka might have been a hell-raiser, but he didn't get into trouble. If you told him to be there at 4:00, he was there at 4:00.

His dad was a steelworker. There were people in that area who said, "Don't take Mike! He's nothing but a trouble-maker. His dad's a union organizer." But the doctors, dentists, and coaches who recruited for Pitt in the Beaver Valley said, "That's crazy; the kid's a great football player."

He wanted to win, but he didn't care about personal glory.

I think he was captain of all the postseason games. Ditka was something. In his senior year, seven of the ten opponents voted for all-opponent teams, and he made all seven! Of the other three, he definitely would have made two; I don't know about the third one. So, if all the teams had voted, he definitely would have made nine out of ten.

In 1959, Syracuse won the national title. The game was over when Art Baker danced into the end zone for one touchdown—he just high-stepped it in. The next year, on the first or second play, Ditka looked Baker over and said, "We're going to see if you do any high-stepping this year," and Pitt beat them 10–0. That was a great Syracuse team—they hadn't lost a game since 1958 and this was late October or November. Pitt upset them 10–0 and Baker didn't do any high-stepping!

When Mike played basketball, the opponents' screens completely disappeared. Pitt played Kentucky one year and gave them a pretty good game. They were setting up the screens, so Ditka went in. The screens parted like the Red Sea; they had probably been belted by him a couple of times before. Adolph Rupp, the legendary Kentucky coach, was screaming, "You're pretty rough out there." And Ditka said, "Well, you've got a bunch of guys who are, too."

During the one year Mike played basketball, I got on the officials at Duke and they kicked me out of the pressroom. Young Mike, on the way back to Pitt, came over and said, "Beano, I'll even that over when we play them in October."

In an earlier life, Ditka was probably Achilles.

I saw Bill Murray (Duke's coach) after the 1959 game and he said, "Our plane looked like a hospital." Ditka had laid out half the team! He wasn't a dirty player. He was just as tough as they come.

He also played baseball at Pitt. You should have seen him—temper, strike out. Ditka had a temper—he's always had a temper—but he would hit the ball a mile sometimes.

In 1963, Ditka made the greatest run in NFL history. It was November 24 at Pitt Stadium. The Bears were losing 17–10, Ditka caught the pass, and four or five guys bounced off him. It was unbelievable, but nobody saw it because the games weren't televised then, because of the Kennedy assassination. But now the play is famous and everybody's seen it, because word got around. The game ended in a tie, but the Bears were fighting to win the division. They won the division and beat the Giants 14–10 in Wrigley Field to win the championship.

In an earlier life, Ditka was probably Achilles—a great, great fighter—and he came back as Mike Ditka. He was unbelievable—he gave one hundred percent in every play.

A SPECIAL CASE
GEORGE KISEDA

George Kiseda wrote for the Pittsburgh Sun Telegraph *during Ditka's college days. He went on to successful stints with the* New York Times *and the* Los Angeles Times.

I only covered Ditka in college; I never had any contact with him after that. I have to admit that I, along with a lot of other writers, didn't realize at the time what a good source Ditka would have been for anecdotes and quotes.

You could tell he was good in college; you didn't have to be that sharp to know that. He played two ways. Instead of a tight end, Army's Red Blaik introduced the "lonely end." The lonely end would split way out wide. Pitt did that with Ditka; he was the lonely end and he was also the punter.

He made the greatest run in NFL history. You can see it every once in a while on NFL highlight films—it was in a game against the Steelers at Forbes Field. If I'm not mistaken, they played the game the weekend that Kennedy was assassinated, and there was a lot of criticism of them for that. He made that unbelievable run after he caught a pass, and he just steamrollered the guys, just ran right over them. It was at least three sure tackles.

I realized he was really different, a special case, after reading about him once he became a pro. When I read about him, I said, "Jeez, this guy's a treasure, and we just weren't on top of it then."

We didn't interview the individual players in those days, in the '50s. One guy was assigned to write the game story and somebody else did the dressing room story. If you were doing the game story, you really didn't even go to the dressing rooms after the game. Now, that would be unheard of; you couldn't hold your job now if you did that.

Bronco Terrell Davis demands that the nameplate above his locker always must read "Joe Abdullah," and Bronco center Tom Maler won't wash his practice gear during the year because he feels that he's giving the equipment "natural seasoning" to shield him from "evil spirits."

A GENEROUS SPEAKER
MAURY YOUMANS

photo courtesy of Maury Youmans

Maury Youmans was a member of Syracuse University's 1959 National Championship team and later enjoyed a fine career with the Chicago Bears and the Dallas Cowboys.

My son was in high school the year the Bears won the Super Bowl, in 1986. He went to a small Catholic school, Saint Petersburg Catholic, and before the Bears won, the school asked me if I could get Mike Ditka to be a speaker. I was pretty sure I couldn't, but I was willing to call and ask him. I congratulated him on winning the playoff game and on going to the Super Bowl, and told him about the banquet the school had planned and asked if he could speak at it. He said no, that he was busy on that date, but that he had two other dates open and if I was willing to switch, he would do it. The school checked and they were able to switch, and then they asked me how much he charged. So I called him up. I said, "Mike, we've arranged the date, and by the way, I don't know what you charge. I'll be glad to send an airline ticket."

He laughed and said, "Maury, you can't afford me. But for you and for the kids, I'll do it for whatever honorarium you can arrange to give me." So I think we gave him $1,000, when he was used to getting $10,000 to $15,000. By then, they had won the Super Bowl, and it couldn't have been better for our group.

I played against him in college but had no idea who he was. We played Pittsburgh my senior year and we trounced them pretty good, but I don't remember him in particular in that game. We were always friends, but we weren't real close. I didn't buddy around with him. He buddied around with Stan Mikita.

I never thought Ditka would coach. But I guess if you spend any time with Landry, and you're willing to assist him, then you've got the basis to be a great NFL coach.

> The 1943 Heisman winner, Angelo Bertelli, started the first six games for Notre Dame, went to boot camp because of World War II, and was replaced by Johnny Lujack. Notre Dame is the only team ever to have two Heisman Trophy winners on the same roster.

Chapter 2

photo courtesy of *Dallas Cowboys Weekly*

Dick Butkus

Doug Buffone

Gale Sayers

Mike Pyle

Gary Ballman

Frank Clarke

Walt Garrison

Donnie Tolbert

Hollywood Henderson

Jim McMahon

Mike Singletary

Players

photo courtesy of the Chicago Bears

A BEAR OF A PARTY
DICK BUTKUS

Dick Butkus was a fullback at a Chicago vocational high school who wanted to attend Notre Dame. When he was told they would not accept married students, Butkus went to the University of Illinois instead and became the greatest player in their history. Butkus joined the Bears in 1965, but his wonderful career with the team was cut short by knee injuries.

One day, I got my first hint that just maybe I was beginning to be accepted by some of the older players. O'Bradovich came over to me on the practice field and said that if I was a good boy I might be invited to Bob Wetoska's birthday party—an annual, semisecret affair held at a local saloon in Rensselaer. The party was not so much to mark another year in Wetoska's life as to celebrate the end of our two-a-day practice hell. Bob was a veteran offensive tackle and a co-captain. I respected him a great deal.

When I joined the veterans at the party later on, I found out that everybody was invited. So much for O'Bradovich's private invitation—and my thinking I was becoming accepted. Strong safety Richie Petitbon was there, along with reserve quarterback Frank Budka, Mike Ditka, defensive end Doug Atkins, and all the other rookies, including running back Brian Piccolo, who never had to go through the ragging I did.

The beer began to flow immediately, and pretty soon someone suggested a drinking contest among the rookies. O'B nominated me to represent the defense because he remembered my high guzzling aptitude from that first semester at Illinois. Somebody picked Piccolo to swig for the offense. This pleased me. It meant payback time for all the snide comments and insults I received from the veterans while Brian usually got off unscathed.

Ditka wrapped his head with a bandanna and declared himself the referee. A table was cleared and two large glasses of beer were set down. Brian and I faced off on either side of the table. Ditka slapped his big mitts, signaling the start, and I drained my glass before Brian barely had his to his lips. Applause and hoots and hollers from the defense rocked the saloon, and the gambling began. Petitbon and O'B bankrolled the effort, and pretty soon I was beating everyone the offense threw at me.

> The Chicago Bears have the most members in the Hall of Fame, with twenty-eight. They have the most wins, with more than six hundred. They have the most numbers retired, with thirteen.

After about an hour of this, I was getting pretty shitfaced. But I was still functioning. Then someone yelled, "Hey! We have to get to our meeting! It's almost seven!"

Chairs scraped back as everyone got up to leave. Everyone except Doug Atkins, that is. He was standing at the door with a bottle of Wild Turkey, informing us that nobody was going anywhere. As big as some of us were, Doug Atkins was in a league by himself. I never saw anybody like Atkins. Nobody ever saw anybody like

Ditka wrapped his head with a bandanna and declared himself the referee.

Atkins. Six-foot-eight, 275 pounds, and not enough fat on him to cook an egg. On top of that, he was not your typical gentle giant. Dougie's exploits were legendary in pro football camps from Baltimore to Oakland.

Finally someone promised him that we would come right back after the meeting, so Doug said, "Well, okay then. But first everyone has to take a swig of this Wild Turkey."

So we all lined up and took our medicine, which did not sit all that well on top of a couple of gallons of beer. I jumped in my Buick Riviera and flew to the local hall where we held our team meetings. As I arrived at the building, I neglected to hit the brakes in a timely manner, and the car stopped halfway up the stairs leading to the front door. I'm lucky I didn't kill anyone. Inside, Frank Budka produced one of those plastic horns the fans use to make noise at games, and he started blowing into it, which got everybody's attention. Happy as hell with himself, he belted out a song:

> Hooray for Halas, hooray at last!
> Hooray for Halas, he's a horse's ass!

Just as Budka was finishing his solo, in walked the old man—with rockets going off in his eyes. He ripped the horn out of Rudy's hand and rapped him over the head with it a couple of times. Then he said in that grating voice, "You son of a bitch! You're drunk! Now quiet down, all of you—you crazy bastards! Break into your groups, NOW!"

Everybody got real quiet and I noticed that Atkins was sitting there in the back, shaking his head in dismay at such juvenile behavior, while up front Papa Bear, with his big hands on his hips, started in again, cursing everybody's mother. Over to one side, George Allen was waiting for the thunder to subside, and I was thinking, "Wow, so this is the NFL!"

When Halas finally calmed down, our defensive unit gathered around Allen. Seeing—and no doubt smelling—our advanced state of intoxication, Allen quickly reduced his syllabus to a few simple points and let us out of school early. We promptly returned to the saloon, but Atkins got there first and took his position at the doorway. Our ticket inside was another swallow of that Wild Turkey.

That was my first of many team parties.

> The Oakland Raiders do not retire numbers.
> Neither do the Dallas Cowboys—but they do put
> the number in a Circle of Honor.

A CERTAIN EDGE
DOUG BUFFONE

Doug Buffone, a native of Yatesboro, Pennsylvania, joined the Chicago Bears in 1966 as a fourth-round draft pick from the University of Louisville. After an outstanding fourteen-year career with the Bears, Buffone quickly became a force in the Chicago sports radio market.

photo courtesy of the Chicago Bears

Both Ditka and I are from western Pennsylvania, where football is king and everything rotates around it. The first time I played against Ditka was prior to the College All-Stars game in 1966. We were playing the Packers that year; the Packers were the champs. We wanted to get tuned up for the Packers, so the All-Stars went down to the Chicago Bears' training camp in Renssalaer, Indiana, to scrimmage the Bears. Of course, I was going to be a Bear after the All-Stars game was over.

We went down and scrimmaged the Bears. I lined up in my outside linebacker position, and of course that position was right on top of the tight end. That tight end was Mike Ditka. It was a hell of a day. It got so damn bad that he started telling me which way the plays were going so we could make a play. The guy was beating me to death; they were running over me and everything else. After the scrimmage was over, I asked myself, "Do I belong in the National Football League?" It was a tough day.

After the scrimmage, we went back to our camp in Evanston. We practiced, we played the Packers, and we got beat. Afterward, I joined the Chicago Bears. I think I was able to become an NFL linebacker, who eventually would play fourteen years, because my first year was pure hell. Can you imagine looking into Ditka's face every day? I was probably the only guy who was happy when he was traded to Philadelphia at the end of that year. We were always fighting—it was World War III every day. Once, in the middle of the season, someone was talking about the opponents, and I heard Ditka say, "Yeah, that fucking Buffone, he gives me more trouble than anybody." That made me feel pretty good because in practice I was going after him. That's the way you have to play if you want to survive. That's why he was Iron Mike.

In '67 and '68, after Mike was traded to Philadelphia, I played against him. By that time I knew him inside and out, and I knew it was going to be a long day. Mike liked to hit people—that was part of being a linebacker. Everyone thought he could catch the ball; I thought he was one of the best blockers around. When he did come out and block you, he was deadly. He would literally come out and drill you. I've played with some of the best, and you have to have this certain edge, this certain attitude, to play the game. You need it to be successful, at least for longevity in the game.

When I heard Ditka was hired in Dallas, I thought, "Look out. He'll put Landry in a booth." In fact, I had Dan Reeves on my radio show and he and I were talking about it. Mike and Dan were two different guys. Mike was wild and tough. Dan Reeves was

> The Chicago Bears wear blue and orange
> because those are the colors that team
> founder George Halas wore when he played
> for the University of Illinois.

also very intense, but he was more of a quiet type—a gentleman. I told Dan Reeves I didn't know how they meshed. Tom Landry was so stoic, standing on the sidelines with his little hat on. Even when it rained, he never got wet. You never got a chance to look at him. Ditka was wild and churlish, but that was something the Dallas Cowboys needed, and I think Tom Landry

Halas knew that Ditka would sell in Chicago. They needed someone with attitude.

realized that. They became great friends. And Ditka and Dan Reeves always had the highest praise for Tom Landry, although everybody thought Tom Landry was a cold fish.

Before I knew Ditka was hired as head coach of the Bears, I got a call from George Allen, who had drafted me in 1966. He had left the Bears after a falling out with George Halas. Allen called and talked to me about how he wanted to be the Bears' new head coach.

At this time, I didn't know anything about Mike Ditka becoming coach of the Bears. So I called George Halas and talked to him about Allen. That's when Halas told me, "I've got to bring back the tradition of the Chicago Bears, bring back the two-fisted, Grabowski-type deal, so I really want Mike Ditka as my head coach." I knew that deep down Halas had an affection for Ditka because they came from the same mold. I honestly believe they are the same person. They have the same attitude, the same toughness. Halas knew that Ditka would sell in Chicago, and he also knew that he had to turn his team around somehow. They needed someone with an attitude. The city needed an emotional lift; I think that's why he went with Mike Ditka.

I started doing radio shows when I retired after the 1979–80 season. Now I have a show on The Score (WSCR) in Chicago with Norm VanLier called "The Bull and the Bear."

Ditka does radio work for us at The Score. Before he left Chicago, he did an hour show on our station every week, so I saw him quite a bit. He also has a restaurant in town, so he goes back and forth a lot.

Chicago loves him because he's a Hall of Famer who played football here on a championship team in 1963, and because he took the team to the Super Bowl in 1985. He represents what the people in this town like about football. It's got to be tough. They want to know that you're going to go out there and knock somebody on their ass, and they want you to win while you're doing it. They want you to be physical and they want you to be tough. That sounds just like Mike Ditka, doesn't it? They fell in love with Ditka, and to this day I get phone calls all the time: "Bring back the Coach. Bring back the Coach."

Quarterback Brad Johnson, who started more games at Florida State in basketball than he did in football, is the only NFL quarterback in history to complete a touchdown pass to himself.

THE TOUGHEST MAN ON THE FIELD
GALE SAYERS

photo courtesy of the Chicago Bears

Gale Sayers was born in Wichita, Kansas, but grew up in Omaha, Nebraska. He is the youngest player ever to be inducted into the Hall of Fame, and also had the shortest career of any inductee, just seven years. Many consider him the greatest running back in NFL history. He now owns Gale Sayers Computer Supplies in Mount Prospect, Illinois.

When I came out of Kansas I didn't know anything about the Bears. I played offense and Mike played offense, but I didn't know anything else about him. I had heard of George Halas, but I didn't know a whole lot about the players. I just wanted to make the ball club. When I got to the Bears, I saw how intense Mike was, and I thought it was great because you have to be that way in pro football.

When I was with the Bears, I never really hung around with Mike that much. Most of the white players lived on the North Side of Chicago, and most of the black players lived on the South Side of Chicago. The only time we saw each other was when we practiced or played a game; we really never saw each other socially unless we attended team parties and things like that. But it wasn't anything like, "We don't want to be around you." It was just the way it happened.

I remember Mike as a very, very tough football player. If you didn't hustle, he would get on your tail. When the game was on

the line, Mike was there. Even when he was hurt, he would take shots in his knees and ankles to play, because Mike Ditka on one leg is better than a second-string tight end on three legs. He always gave 110 percent on every play—he was a tremendous football player.

Dick Butkus was also a tough player; he played every down like it was the last down. It was the same with Mike—he played every down like it was the last, and he would block, catch passes, and do anything he could to win a football game. This is what I admired about him.

Sometime in their pasts, somebody— whether a parent, a high school coach, or a college coach—told them, "If you want to be a great player, you have to go out all the way on every play." Somebody said to them, "Hey, if you're going to be great, you can't do it half the time, or three plays out of four, or two plays out of four; you have to do it every play." Somebody told them that, just like somebody told me that. My grade school coach said, "Gale, you've got a lot of talent, but you have to use it. You have to prepare yourself, because if you don't, you'll waste your talent." I really believe that somebody told them, "Hey, you have to be the toughest man on the field," and they believed that. I know Dick believed that, and I'm pretty sure Mike believed that, too.

I was very surprised to find out that Tom Landry had hired Mike as an assistant. When Landry hired Mike, it was the beginning of the end of hard-nosed coaches grabbing your helmet and cussing you out. Mike was the end of that era; he could still do that to some of his players. Today you can't do that.

When the game was on the line, Mike was there.

Will he be successful at New Orleans? I don't know. He sold the house when he got Ricky Williams, so I hope he is successful, because he's going to be gone if he's not. If Williams does get hurt, Mike's in real trouble. You can say what you want about Mike. He's probably a good coach and a good motivator, but you still have to have talented players; it's as simple as that. I don't care how good of a motivator you are, if the people on the field don't have the talent, you're not going to be a good coach.

The Los Angeles Rams were the first NFL team to wear helmets with a logo. The logo was designed by a player, Fred Gehrke. The Cleveland Browns are the only team with no logo.

photo courtesy of the Chicago Bears

DITKA THE GRABOWSKI
MIKE PYLE

Mike Pyle and Mike Ditka both joined the Bears as rookies in 1961 and were roommates the night before every Bears away game, until Ditka was traded to the Eagles for Jack Concannon in 1967. Pyle was a well-established radio personality in Chicago by the time Ditka returned fifteen years later to guide the Bears. That commenced a ten-year-long relationship as Pyle hosted Ditka's "Coaches' Show" during Ditka's entire reign.

ROOMIES

Ditka and I were roommates on the road from the time we both joined the Bears in 1961 until he was traded to the Philadelphia Eagles in 1967. There were three of us coming from the All-Star camp, so at least two of us were going to room together, and somehow the draw paired Mike and I. I got along well with Mike and I think he got along well with me, and it stayed that way for the six years that Mike played for the Bears. What an interesting combination—a guy from Winnetka who went to Yale and a guy from Aliquippa who went to Pittsburgh. But we were friends right from the start.

I never heard of Ditka when I was in college. I first heard of him when the Bears drafted him in the first round and drafted me in the seventh round. We played college football for four years at the same time, but the Pittsburgh teams weren't great teams and I was an Ivy Leaguer.

I only remember one time that Ditka came out on the wrong side of a scuffle. It was in Sonoma, California, where we would practice, between the San Francisco and LA games. There were no big jets in those days to fly us home in between games. One day in practice, Mike ran a pattern against the backups who ran the plays of the team we were going to play. He thought the safety, Don Mullins, had held him or something, and he charged him. But Mullins was a safety and pretty quick, and all he did was sidestep Ditka and get his fist inside that stupid single-bar helmet Ditka always wore. Ditka caused the impact; he ran into the fist. Forty guys fell dead silent as Ditka went down to his knees, but didn't collapse. He got up and went back to the huddle. He said, "I got whupped!" Can you imagine what the media in Chicago would do with a story like that nowadays?

BYE-BYE BIRDIE

I went to high school with Ann-Margret Olsen. In high school, she was a beautiful young girl. I knew her well, but she wasn't a part of my group. Several guys in my class dated girls in her class—her best friends. But she wasn't as popular as she could have been; her parents were from Sweden, and they were really tough.

When Ditka and I were rookies with the Bears in '61, we went to LA for our first game. I don't think I'd ever been to LA before. Ann-Margret was in LA because she didn't finish at Northwestern; George Burns discovered her and took her out there. When I arrived, I called one of my New Trier classmates, Tom, who was in the Marine Corps at Camp Pendleton. He came over and picked me up where we were staying in LA. I couldn't get Ann-Margret's phone number, but I had her apartment number. We drove over to see her, and her mother was there. Ann was making "Bye-Bye Birdie" in Dallas at the time. Tom and I had to sit and talk with Mrs. Olsen for three hours. It was not what we had planned.

The next year, I called her. Halas had us staying in Long Beach—forty miles from where she lived. I was really lucky this time. I got her on the phone, but I didn't get to see her because we had meetings. So I offered her a couple of game tickets and she said, "Sure."

She came to the game with a starlet friend. After the game, I came out of the locker room at the Coliseum, and she was there. She threw her arms around me, gave me a kiss, and introduced me to her friend. I had to get on a bus to leave, so we walked up the ramp at

> Q: Which Heisman Trophy winner made the most money?
> A: 1959 winner Billy Cannon of LSU. A successful dentist, he nevertheless spent several years in jail for counterfeiting.

photo courtesy of Mike Pyle

Walter Payton, Mike Ditka, and Mike Pyle

the Coliseum. This is when Mike Pyle became a veteran. I was still a rookie until after this game, when the rest of the team saw me kissing Ann-Margret goodbye at the bus door. Then Ann-Margret and her friend walked around the bus and it almost tipped over. From then on, I was a veteran.

I talked to Ann-Margret about a year ago. She's extremely nice. She never forgot where she came from, which is good.

THE REAL STORY

In his autobiography, Ditka tells a story I know very well, about staying out after curfew at training camp. In the book, Mike said I was the guy who ran into a wire fence, but it was Ditka. I'll tell the story the correct way.

We'd been forced to come back early from a preseason game just so Halas could get us back in camp, because he wanted to know where everybody was. The whole team was madder than hell. A handful of us went to Brook Country Club, where you could get a beer on Sunday; you couldn't do that anywhere else in Indiana. Rick Casares, Ditka, Roger Davis, Richie Petitbon, myself, and a few other players were there. We were mad, and we started bitching about how Halas treated us and what he made us do. We were getting madder and madder, and drinking more and more. Several guys said, "We've got to go back to training camp." But Ditka, Petitbon, Casares, and I decided not to go back. It got to be 12:00, and the club closed up. We drove back to camp in Rich Casares's Lincoln. Ditka said—and this is the truth—"We're going to get caught by the Silver Bullet (a retired cop who spied on the team for Halas)."

> **I don't think Ditka has ever felt pain; I don't think he even has a pain threshold.**

It was me or Richie Petitbon who said, "Let's sneak into the cafeteria." We were hungry since we hadn't had dinner, so we decided to break into the cafeteria. Ditka said, "I'm not going to break into the cafeteria." He jumped out of the car, ran across the field to our dorm, and ran into the wire. If I had run into that wire, I would have woken up everyone in the place, because I don't like pain. I don't think Ditka has ever felt pain; I don't think he even has a pain threshold.

When I saw Ditka the next day, it looked like he had cut his legs off running full speed into the wire. He was the guy who ran into the wire, not me. The three of us sneaked into the cafeteria, ate a bunch of food, and went back to the dorm.

That night, when we came back and parked after Ditka ran out of the car, the Bullet saw three people in Casares's car. The next day,

Halas called everybody up after practice and said, "You know, some of your teammates don't have much respect for the rest of the team. There were three guys who stayed out after curfew last night. They really don't have much respect for the rest of you. There were three people, but I only know whose car it was, and your buddy Rick Casares doesn't have much respect for you guys. The other two guys don't either; I'm going to fine Rick Casaras $1,500 and see if he has any friends."

When we broke and started heading for the locker room, I ran up to Richie Petitbon. I said to Rich, "Let's go have some fun with Rick." So Richie and I ran up to Casares. We said, "Rick, that's really too bad. Who were the other two guys?" He just laughed. Later, I asked Rick if he ever got fined that $1,500, because sometimes, if we had a good season, Halas would forgive those fines. But Rick said, "Yeah." And I said, "Rick, I owe you money." He said, "Don't worry about it. I wouldn't take it if you gave it to me." That's the kind of guy he was.

THE CAST

Mike rarely played in training camp. The rest of us would play a lot and be tired going into the season; we'd really have to work hard to get some spring back in our legs because training camp was so tough. But since Mike did everything at full speed, he was generally hurt during training camp.

If Ditka stayed out at night, he worked harder the next day. He worked hard to pay the fiddler, and as a result, he probably had more strains and pulled muscles than most guys. The rest of us

> Joe Theismann holds the NFL record for the shortest punt that wasn't blocked—one yard.

might try to ease up a little bit if we had a hangover or felt bad, but Mike would have a lot of injuries because he worked as hard as he could work.

One year—I think it was his first year—he hurt his foot. The doctors put a cast on it and told him he couldn't practice for three to four weeks. After about two weeks, Mike cut the cast off himself, went out, and started practicing. He ended up breaking his arch, and he missed three or four games. That was the most amazing thing I ever saw—Mike cutting his own cast off to go out and practice. Pain did not get in his way.

I think Mike would agree that cutting off that cast and breaking his arch probably caused his first hip replacement. I've talked to Mike about it over the years. He started running in Dallas, and then went into an absolute fitness craze right at the end of his career. He was getting older like everyone does—he wasn't as quick and he was losing some of his skills. So he went on a fitness tear, and the weight loss from the running probably kept him in the game a year or two longer. He continued to run when he was coaching, and it got to the point where he would run five or six miles, seven days a week. He and Diana once joined my wife and I and a couple of other couples in Aspen, and he would get up, run four miles, and then ski all day. We all thought he was absolutely nuts. Well, it turned out that running on that bad foot for all those years led to him destroying his hip and needing a hip replacement. I was able to track the damage back to when he cut his cast off as a rookie.

In the early part of the twentieth century, a college football game was seventy minutes long and five yards got you a first down.

CO-CAPTAINS

When Ditka and I were rookies together in 1961, the NFL was just beginning to gain fame. The NFL's growth really became accepted by the public during the fifties. The 1958 championship game in New York that the Colts won in overtime was the beginning of a period of recognition for the National Football League. National publicity, like the TV show "The Violent World of Sam Huff," began after that '58 game.

So Ditka and I came in right at the beginning of the real growth of the National Football League. It was an interesting time, because the game was growing in popularity, but we still played exhibition games in those little towns. We didn't have full stadiums. We had full crowds at Wrigley Field, but even in the early '60s the league

As wild as Ditka is on the outside, he's got the strongest motivational, inspirational, and competitive core of any man I've ever known.

was changing. Around the time I started, a rule was passed that a stadium had to have a minimum of 55,000 or 60,000 seats. We never could put more than 45,000 in Wrigley Field, but the NFL let Halas play there until 1970 because he was the founder of the league.

In 1971, Halas and the Bears were forced to go to Soldier Field, which is the worst stadium in the league. It was built for a World's Fair, not for anything competitive. It was built with 112,000 seats along the sidelines, for which you would have to have a three-hundred-yard football field. It was just an odd stadium that wasn't built around a football field. It is better now; they've rebuilt it many times, but even with all the rebuilding it's still the worst stadium in pro football. When people ask why I say that, it's because it's a shallow stadium. If you sit low on the fifty-yard line, you can't see over the crown on the field. If you sit high, even though they're probably the best seats, you are a mile from the field. It's not bad from the players' point of view; there is a nice field, but it's not a durable field. Any bad weather will really mess it up.

I was the captain of the team for seven of my nine years. During the 1963 training camp, George Halas asked both Ditka and I if we'd be the co-captains of the offensive team. That was the year we won the championship, and it was Mike's and my first year as co-captains for the offense. Mike was a captain until he left in 1967, and I was a captain until I left after 1969. The two previous captains—linebacker Bill George and Stan Jones on offense—had been captains for many years. Halas went to four captains. We never had elections; we were just appointed.

As wild as Ditka is on the outside, he's got the strongest motivational, inspirational, and competitive core of any man I've ever known. I've known guys who've played with the same intensity, but I think Mike is the best.

Mike got into a contract argument with George Halas. Mike always represented himself; none of us had agents in those days. Halas wouldn't talk to an agent. Ditka told a newspaper writer that Halas threw nickels around like manhole covers, and the writer printed it. It's a wonderful line, but right after it was printed, Halas traded him. But Ditka still had plenty of playing left. And it sure wasn't a good trade.

> The first Super Bowl, in 1967 at the Los Angeles
> Coliseum, had 32,000 empty seats even
> though the most expensive ticket
> was $12.00, not $275.00 like it is today.

THE RADIO SHOW

I hosted a radio show with Mike the whole time he was in Chicago. A lot of people thought that would be the end of my radio career, because when you're the moderator and you've got one of the best-known sports celebrities in America, you can't have a personality on the show. The general manager of the station said I was doing the wrong thing by hosting the Ditka show, but I loved doing it because Ditka and I had been friends for a long time, and I made more money working with Ditka. The station manager said, "You know the game of football, but you'll never be able to express an opinion when you've got Ditka as the master." But I made more money with Ditka than if I had my own show and could say, "Ditka's right" or "Ditka's wrong."

In 1987, there was a bitter players' strike. I was the president of the NFL Players' Association when we registered with the National Labor Relations Board in the winter of 1968. During the strike I would ask my questions, and obviously I was a strong supporter of the players' side. Mike, like always, was not diplomatic, and he'd get mad at me and we'd argue on the air. It was good radio, but if that had not have happened, the players might not have been as mad at him. Mike would publicly give his opinion on the air, and I loved generating it because I knew quite a bit about the other side. Ditka's position wasn't popular with the players, but how in the hell could they fight his position—how can a group of employees fight an employer who pays people that much money to do what they love to do?

He just said, "Don't tell me about all these other issues—free agency, equitable treatment, and all the other things that the union would argue and fight for. Why would you ever want to interrupt or disturb people who pay you that much to do what you love to do most?"

I felt his philosophy was oversimplified, and we sure had some interesting shows because of that. But today I believe that Mike's more right than I am. I'm turning the corner, because the game of football is nowhere near as good as it was a few years ago. It's not as enjoyable. The games are not as much fun with so many players changing teams every year.

Ditka is still extremely popular in Chicago because he's one of those unique celebrity personalities who's hard to get to know. It's the Grabowski thing—he really hit a chord with his behavior and actions. That is what the Midwest is about, and he wouldn't be as popular in New York City or Los Angeles. He's a Midwestern, provincial Chicago Grabowski. Once you like a Midwesterner, you like him forever.

Ditka's position wasn't popular with the players, but how in the hell could they fight his position?

Normally, our show was on Monday nights, but one time the Bears played the Monday night before Election Day and we did the show on Tuesday night. For some reason, we had to pretape it; we weren't doing it live, and we couldn't take phone calls. So I had to change the format if I wasn't going to take phone calls. I could have talked to Mike for an hour, but I thought I would try to make it better. So I got George Connors and Doug Buffone to come into the studio. I was trying to get players from different eras, so I got Roland Harper, a younger guy who started in 1975 with Payton, on the phone. As I recall, Roland Harper said about two things because Doug Buffone, who played with Ditka, and George Connors ("Mr. Chicago") took over. Doug said "Mike, in the game yesterday, you had a player who didn't call an audible and instead ran a play that couldn't be run against the particular defense that had been called. You couldn't run that play against that defense. Why didn't the quarterback change that play?"

Now, this was insider stuff. Doug's the only guy who would have recognized that defense. Mike used to yell at callers—that's why he was so good on the radio. When callers would ask stupid questions, Ditka would say, "That's a stupid question and I'm not going to answer it." That was great radio. But in this case, he said, "You know, Doug, you're right." I never heard Ditka tell a person asking a question that he was right. He said "You're right, he should have called an audible." Doug was so happy that he said, "Maybe part of your game plan was wrong." Then everyone was talking offense and defense and getting the coach to tell them how the offenses and plays are designed, and why they were in the game plan. I was personally fascinated.

> **Ditka would say, "That's a stupid question and I'm not going to answer it."**

Both Harry Caray and Mike Ditka had the ability not to be diplomatic and the courage to say what they thought. I think that's the reason for Mike's popularity. The other guys, the Brickhouses of the world, were always being careful.

The last year we did the show, the season was going badly. We were on the Score radio (WSCR), and we had to have the Score guys on every week. They were doing it to get rid of me, and they did, when Mike was fired. They typed me as a WGN man, a company man, an easy man who never got tough. When we did the show on WMAQ, they hired Chet Coppock and asked if I minded if he was on the show.

So I had to use Chet on the air with Ditka. Chet felt this was a platform for him to get tough with the coach, and he'd ask these tough questions. Mike would say, "I don't want to answer that," or he would direct an answer to Chet, and not to the audience. I would defend my style with the media, the fans, and everyone else.

They called me a company man and said I asked easy questions. I asked questions that Mike Ditka answered. I thought my job was to get as much information about the Chicago Bears and his coaching techniques as I could. To me, that's the mission of a radio interviewer. No, I didn't get credited with asking a tough question, but I didn't need that. I was trying to get information on the Bears and on what Mike Ditka was doing. When we had the show on WGN, the managers would tell me that I shouldn't do the show because I didn't get to talk about what I knew about the Bears and the game. I said, "Well, that's a concession I make. If I wanted to sit here and argue with Ditka, I don't think Ditka would want me as the moderator. Mike isn't trying to be a radio star. He gets paid a bunch of money and he knows it's in his best interest to communicate with the fans. That's the reason he's doing it. Does he want to argue with me on the radio?" That's what the Chet Coppocks, the Mike Norths, and the other guys do.

I moved the show to the Score. The Score wanted it and it was the best show they had on the air in 1992, the last season Ditka coached the Bears. As part of the deal, the Score wanted their guys on the air. The Score guys would sit behind me while I tried to control the show. I would try to steer Mike on to something that went on in the game the day before. The guys sitting behind me would interrupt my question line because they wanted to get all the air time. I'd give them the standard radio hand signals, and they would not take my signals. I hated the experience because I didn't like any of the guys on the Score. If that's talk radio, then I'm going to plant flowers or get in another business.

> The Packers have sold out every game since 1960 and at $30 have the lowest average ticket price in the NFL.

My favorite radio story about Ditka took place while we were doing the Ditka show with Chet Coppock on WMAQ. I would do two or three shows every summer at training camp. The radio station would send an engineer and equipment up, and I would do a show with Ditka in his office after practice. It was always a fun show and a relaxed atmosphere. One year, we had a little trouble taking phone calls since I was the only one doing the show in Platteville. We had to have someone in the studio in Chicago answer the phones and hang them up. Chet said he would take care of the phones. I got on the phone with Chet before the show and said, "Chet, I want you to know that I'm the guy who interviews Mike on this program. You're going to have control of the microphones in Chicago. I don't want you to do all the talking. Yes, I need you to answer the phones. You can ask your questions as you normally do, but it's my show. I want to control it."

The show started and Chet was just carrying on. About two minutes into his carrying on, my wife pulled a deck of cards out of her purse, looked at Mike and looked at me, and we both nodded "yes." I took the deck of cards. I was the moderator of the show. Ditka was the star of the show. I dealt a hand of gin. Mike and I, during the first half hour of the show, played three hands of gin while Chet talked. Occasionally Mike would have to answer a question. I'd have to do a commercial cue or ask a question, but we played three hands of gin in Mike's office in Platteville while Coppock carried on and wouldn't give us the microphone.

In 1992, Ditka was angry most of the time because he was being criticized by the press and his team wasn't winning. He was coaching a team that had been totally dismantled by McCaskey. He had had a great team that had won the championship in '85, and had only had a couple of bad playoff games because of injured quarterbacks in '86 and '87. He could have easily won three championships. It wasn't that he was a bad coach. With Jim McMahon hurt going into the playoffs in '86 and '87, they weren't going to win a championship. With McMahon they might have. But everybody said his coaching wasn't any good.

> **Getting fired was the best thing that could have happened to Mike at the time.**

Ditka would never admit that he didn't have the talent to win. He kept wanting to win and it really hurt him that he couldn't. It created a stress and an inability to coach as well, because he was still trying to be good with less talent. It wasn't Mike's fault. It was the guy who owned and dismantled the team. When Wilber Marshall went to the Redskins for $6 million, there were fourteen unsigned players, of which seven or eight were starters. Anybody who could spell football could have made that deal and gotten Marshall away from the Bears. They knew the Bears wouldn't match it. You don't pay a guy like Wilber Marshall $6 million in 1986 and 1987 and have fourteen other guys unsigned. But McCaskey hadn't taken care of business, and that's why Wilber Marshall left. Then he lost Willie Gault because he argued with him about a little money, and he lost Otis Wilson. He lost one guy after another because of mismanagement, and Ditka was trying to win with a terrible team. So he was mad.

Getting fired was the best thing that could have happened to Mike at the time. The Bears were a bad football team and Mike was one of the most popular sports celebrities in the country. He still does a radio show in Chicago and he's in his third year as coach of the New Orleans Saints. Now that's blind loyalty.

DITKA THE MAN

Ditka is good at golf; he can hit the ball far, but he really works on the short game. And he's got a great touch. That's why he could play to a five handicap. I don't know what his handicap is now with his leg problems. I've watched him work at it—he chips and putts and works on the fine game all the time. He's totally committed. He'd spend ten hours a day in the winter at Bob O'Link at their indoor range hitting golf balls. That's how you get good.

My wife and I hosted a birthday party for Mike every year. It was a fun party with lots of funny gifts. Once, at around the fifth year, Diana showed up and Ditka wasn't there. Diana got mad and called Bob O'Link. The man at Bob O'Link said, "He doesn't want to be interrupted, Mrs. Ditka." So Diana made me call. I called and got the same thing. I said, "Give him a message, please." He was three hours late for his own birthday party.

The next year, Candy and I decided that everybody would wear the same thing—a shirt that said something like "Another Year, Same Shit." We'd even gotten one for Diana. Ditka, after arriving late, got a shirt, too, but his said "The Big Shit."

Because of his competitiveness, Mike doesn't take practical joking well. So he's the best guy to play a practical joke on. He doesn't laugh it off easily.

Neill Armstrong ended his four-year head coaching stint with the Bears at the end of the 1981 season. He was not an inspirational coach, but he was a very smart and a neat guy, and I loved him. I did the radio show with him every year he coached. He was a good coach, but he didn't have that motivational, inspirational energy. If you're a sports coach, one of the most important things you have to do is make sure that your players are giving everything they have, and that they're not taking anything home with them. Well, he had

Mike Ditka's life expectancy in war or combat would be about a second and a half, because that's the only speed he knows.

a team that didn't care and didn't leave everything on the field, so I knew they had to do something, and Ditka was the kind of guy they needed. He'd never even been a coordinator, but he had respect for George Halas and a love of Chicago and the Chicago Bears' tradition. That's why he was absolutely the best choice they could have made. The team had a bunch of guys who might have had the potential to be good players, but they weren't mentally tough. Ditka knew how to make them that.

The first years were fun. I could tell what had happened in a game by listening to his press conference after the game. If he was mad or he yelled, I could tell he was the guy who had made the mistakes. The more he yelled about the things that happened, the more he was covering up for his inability to admit that he might have made a mistake or done something wrong.

He can admit he screwed up and mean it. He does it regularly. He's very capable of humility. When he admits he made a mistake, he means it and will stand by it, but it may not be for forty-eight hours or so. The first time the Bears played the Dallas Cowboys after he joined the team as head coach in '82, something happened in the first half and I thought Mike had screwed up. I wasn't sure, but after listening to the postgame interview and hearing him bitch about the

The Arizona Cardinals are the only NFL team to play in a college stadium— Arizona State's Sun Devil Stadium.

things they did, I said, "It was Mike's fault." I could tell by the way he bellowed and screamed at everybody. He got mad at the media, got mad at the press, got mad at the team. He got mad at everybody. It was because Landry beat him, because Landry outcoached him.

I realized the level of Ditka's intensity as a competitor—not just as an athlete, but in everything he does—the first time I saw him compete. I saw that at the All-Star camp in '61. The next closest in intensity would probably be Dick Butkus. You could make an argument that Butkus was as intense or even more intense than Mike. The only way I've ever been able to describe it is that Mike Ditka's life expectancy in war or combat would be about a second and a half, because that's the only speed he knows.

There are lot of guys with that kind of competitiveness who aren't big enough or strong enough or fast enough to play on the big-time teams. Probably the biggest mistake the NFL makes in scouting players today is not giving enough importance to character. They've got all those rating methods, but I still think they make a big mistake in not judging character. To Ditka, character is very important and has brought guys in that most thought couldn't be players. It's not how big and strong and fast you are, it's how big your heart is. "Are you a football player?"—that's the question. Football is not an easy game to play because you've got to have skills and you've got to have brains. You've got to be smart to play football.

Q: How did the San Diego Chargers get their name?
A: The Chargers were originally the Los Angeles Chargers in 1960, the first year of the AFL. They were owned by Barron Hilton of the Hilton Hotel chain. Hilton owned the Carte Blanche credit card company and named the team to promote the card.

photo courtesy of *Dallas Cowboys Weekly*

IN THE WRONG PLACE AT THE WRONG TIME
GARY BALLMAN

Gary Ballman played with Ditka in Philadelphia in 1967 and 1968.

I first met Mike when NY Giant Andy Robestelli put twelve guys together—me, Ron Kramer, Mike Ditka, and nine others—to do marketing stuff for Allied Chemical Corporation. They had about six different divisions and we would sign autographs and go to banquets as guest speakers.

I was an end and an outside receiver for the Eagles. I was happy to see Ditka come to Philly. He had just had an operation on his foot and he wasn't the same guy, though he had a very high tolerance for pain.

Once, our trainer used some kind of weird detergent and we all had jock rash. We were up in Reading, Pennsylvania. There were hooks in the locker room that came down from the ceiling for drying out uniforms and stuff. They gave us some of this stuff to put on the rash. It burned like you wouldn't believe. Mike was standing beneath the hooks, and he put that stuff on and jumped up and hit a hook. He needed about six stitches in his head. It was the most injury he had that season. He just happened to be in the wrong place at the wrong time.

One time I played golf with Mike at Bala Country Club in Philadelphia. I was getting my woods refinished so I was just hitting irons. We were playing a $5 Nassau and he got so pissed off he threw his clubs in the lake. I never saw a guy as competitive as Mike—he hates to lose.

I didn't think Mike had the temperament to be a head coach. But he's a very bright guy. After he was traded to the Cowboys, I was traveling through Dallas and I gave him a call. We went out to lunch and he told me that he had learned more at Dallas than he ever would have thought. At that time, Dallas was *the* team. Ditka said he learned more from Landry and from their system than from everywhere else combined.

> The Bengals, owned by Paul Brown, were named after the Massillon (Ohio) High School Tigers, whom Brown coached before he became head coach of Ohio State and the Cleveland Browns.

Mike Ditka   photo courtesy of *Dallas Cowboys Weekly*

ON THE LOOKOUT
FRANK CLARKE

*Clarke, a Beloit, Wisconsin, native, spent eleven years in the NFL
as an outstanding receiver, primarily with the Dallas Cowboys.*

In '62 I was on the verge of breaking a seventeen-games-in-
a-row touchdown record. I had fourteen games in a row with
three games to go, and in a game against Washington I got
hurt. I was coming down to block the linebacker, and the guy
viciously kneed me in the thigh with all his force, giving me
severe internal bleeding.

I was still on the sidelines when the Giants beat us, and I also had to miss the next game when we lost to the Bears by a point. I watched from the sidelines as Dandy Don Meredith played a great game, throwing four touchdown passes. The other thing I remember from that game was seeing the Bears' Mike Ditka catch passes and look for people to run over. He was amazing. I never saw any receiver catch the ball and look for people to run over. Of course, you pay the price when you want that kind of contact. At the end of his career, he could hardly walk.

When offered the coaching job at Marshall University, Bobby Bowden changed his mind at the last minute and turned it down. Less than two years later, the entire Marshall staff and team were killed in a plane crash. A few years later, he had a similar change of heart with LSU. LSU's next choice was Bo Rein.

A few months after taking the job, Rein used a private jet on a recruiting trip to Shreveport, Louisiana. On the return leg of the flight, the pilot and Rein were overcome by fumes and the plane flew pilotless across the southeastern United States before running out of gas and crashing into the Atlantic Ocean near Bermuda, killing Rein and the pilot.

photo courtesy of *Dallas Cowboys Weekly*

THE MONK
WALT GARRISON

The pride of Lewisville, Texas, and Oklahoma State University, Walt Garrison began his nine-year pro career with the Cowboys in 1968, one year before Ditka joined the team. He became successful on the rodeo circuit after his football career ended.

Getting Ditka, a future Hall of Famer with a reputation for bloodlust, to play for the Cowboys was Tom Landry's idea. A few days after the '69 season, Tom Landry called Ditka, who had been feuding with Philadelphia coach Joe Kuharich while spending much of his season with the Eagles drinking heavily. Ditka was thinking about retiring, even though he still had a year left on his contract.

Landry told him, "We don't even know if you can play anymore, but we're going to bring you down and take a look at you and see if you can play a few more years." Ditka had always hated the Cowboys because of their arrogance and their goody-two-shoes image, but he despised Kuharich more, and agreed to come if Landry could swing a trade for him. Just prior to the '69 season, the Cowboys shipped Dave McDaniels, a second-round draft choice who turned out to be one of Gil Brandt's mistakes, to Philadelphia in exchange for the eight-year veteran.

Ditka created headlines a week before the '69 season began when he was involved in an early-morning accident after a night on the town. He weighed 235 pounds, and because of his fat jowls halfback Walt Garrison started calling him "Monk," short for "Chipmunk." Garrison, who enjoyed watching a good train wreck, was fascinated by the unpredictable Ditka.

TAUNTING DITKA

When Ditka joined the Cowboys, defensive backs Charlie Waters and Cliff Harris used to taunt him: "Yeah, Mike, you've got some great moves." And they'd swivel their heads back and forth indicating the extent of Ditka's "moves."

In practice, Charlie and Cliff would cover Monk like paint. They'd be all over him because he couldn't beat them deep and they knew it. So they didn't have to be honest. Ditka was slower than the last day of school. He would try his damnedest when he was running his routes to get those two little bastards up close enough so he could give them a forearm to the chops. Right before he made his cut, he'd try to cream our cornerbacks.

That was Ditka.

LIKE PULLING TEETH

Ditka got his teeth knocked out in an auto accident the year he joined us. He flipped his car over a parked car, went through the windshield, and broke his jaw.

The dentist told Ditka, "We can wire your teeth shut, but you can't play tomorrow. Or we can pull them."

Ditka said, "Pull the sonuvabitches."

As it turned out, they had to wire his jaw shut anyway because it was broken. But he played all the same. You could hear him out on the field breathing through his teeth. "Hiss-haw, hiss-haw, hiss-haw"—he sounded like a rabid hound. You could hear that mad dog Ditka cussing even with his mouth wired shut: "God da otherrucker."

Man, that Ditka was mean. He walked into a restaurant one night, walked over to a table with some chairs stacked on it, raked them all off with his big old forearm, and motioned for us to come on over and sit down.

Nobody said a word. I know why, too. Ditka had the foulest temper of any man I've ever met. It was so bad people used to get him mad just to see what he'd do. He could lose control in a slim second and anything could happen. That was the fun of it—the element of surprise.

PANDEMONIUM, DITKA-STYLE

Ditka was a madman. It was always a circus when Mike would play cards. He had a terrible temper when he played cards; he'd even throw chairs across the room. He was a bad card player who hated to lose, and he had a terrible temper. Put them all together, and you've got pandemonium, Ditka-style.

They let him play because before he got mad, he'd lose all his money. He was so competitive he'd stick with lousy cards, and everyone knew it. It was like having your own personal ATM machine.

> During Super Bowl III, when the Jets upset the Baltimore Colts, Joe Namath did not attempt a pass in the 4th quarter.

We usually played a card game called boo-ray before a game, and of course Monk would lose his ass and get so mad he'd start throwing chairs across the room. Hell, Ditka was throwing chairs when Bobby Knight over at

It was always a circus when Mike would play cards.

Indiana University was still using his to sit in. Ditka's big ol' chipmunk cheeks would turn red. Then he'd take the deck of cards and tear them in half and throw the sonuvabitches in the air like confetti.

Lee Roy Jordan would say, "Well, it looks like the game's over."

"Game ain't over till I get a chance to win this money back," Ditka would scream.

Ditka would stay in a hand and try to beat you when he had nothing, and everybody knew it. He was so competitive he wanted to win even if he had an eight-high nothing. As soon as he got pissed off, he'd bet and bet no matter what he had. And we all knew it.

All you could hear through the halls at night was Ditka screaming. You knew Monk was losing again.

They played mostly for markers in camp. Then at the end of camp they'd settle up. By the end of camp, Ditka didn't have any money, of course, and he owed thousands. There was no way he could pay it all. He owed one guy $1,200, another guy $1,500, another guy $2,000. And so he'd go up to each guy and say, "How much on the dollar would you like? Twenty cents on the dollar? I mean, how much actual cash will you take for what I owe you? No way I can pay twelve hundred."

The funny thing is that nobody was really pissed off. The money came so easy from Monk, if they got twenty cents on the dollar it was better than winning straight from somebody else.

Lee Roy Jordan was the only guy who was really upset about the transactions. Lee Roy was smart. He wouldn't drink, he'd just sit there and play his cards while everybody else was drunk as hell, screaming and yelling, laughing and swearing. And, of course, Lee Roy was eating them up.

He was so competitive he'd stick with lousy cards, and everyone knew it. It was like having your own personal ATM machine.

Once, Buddy Dial was out a grand to Lee Roy, Chuck Howley owed him a bunch, and Monk, of course, had signed over his mortgage and his first-born child.

The gambling got so bad that when it came time for the first exhibition game, players were more concerned about who was going to get cut and leave without paying than they were about the team. Guys would be trying to make another player look good just so Landry wouldn't cut his ass and take their winnings with him.

Landry got pissed off one time about the gambling, so he got up in a meeting and said, "No more cards. No more gambling. It's disrupting the team."

So we all went back to our rooms after the meeting and decided that since nobody would get a chance to win any money back, all bets were off. We were going to just tear up all the "owsies."

Lee Roy tore up $5,000 or $6,000 worth of IOU's. And five days later the sonuvabitches were playing again. Why not? They suddenly had all this money saved up that they hadn't lost yet.

YOU CAN GET HURT PLAYING THIS GAME

(Dan) Reeves and (Dave) Manders played Landry and Ditka in tennis one evening at training camp at the apartments at Cal Lutheran, where a lot of young couples go with their kids. Everything was real nice and sociable until Ditka got behind. Then he started up. "S--t! How did I miss that shot! I hate this game!" He was yelling at the top of his lungs, and mothers were scattering around, trying to get their kids out of earshot. They might as well have moved them to Arizona as loud as Ditka was cussing.

The whole time Landry never said a word. Finally, Ditka missed a shot, slammed his racket down, smashed it all to hell, and threw what was left of it at the net. Well, the damn thing went under the net, skipped along the court, and hit Landry in the ankles. Tom was hopping around, hurting like hell, and he looked over at Reeves and said, "Boy, you can get hurt playing this game."

I used to go golfing with Ditka and Reeves and Dave Edwards. Mike threw his club after about every shot. He used to throw stuff all over. I'd just started playing golf, and I thought it was part of the game: get mad, throw a club, cuss, beat your club on the ground, break the damn thing, throw it in the lake—I thought that was how you played golf.

Monk would throw a club over in the woods and I'd go on over there and get it and put it in my bag. That's how I got my first set of clubs.

> Troy Aikman wrote a book which had nothing to do with football. It was a kids' book called *Things Change*, and it sold an astonishing 200,000 copies.

LUCIFER ON WHEELS

A group of the Cowboys started riding motorcycles. On Mondays after the game, we'd usually go to Grapevine Lake and ride out in the dirt all day. Ditka bought a 125cc. Yeah, Ditka was a madman.

> **Ditka was a madman. He bought a yellow Yamaha, but that didn't fit Mike's image of himself so he painted it black.**

He bought a yellow Yamaha, but that didn't fit Mike's image of himself so he painted it black. He bought a black leather jacket and black leather pants and a black helmet. Man, he looked like Lucifer on wheels. The only problem was that he couldn't ride worth beans. The place where we used to go riding a lot had a hill with a creek at the bottom. Monk would always try to jump the creek, and every time he'd miss and hit the other bank. BAM! "Goddamnit!" He'd start that thing up again, go back, and try to jump it again. BAM! "Goddamnit!" He'd get up and go again. BAM! "Goddamnit!"

But what really pissed Ditka off was that Cliff and Charlie could hop that creek like it was a puddle, and they'd yell back at Mike, "Come on, you fat chipmunk!" and ride off. Ditka hated those two little bastards, so he'd go back and BAM! "Goddamnit!"

A few years later, we were playing St. Louis at Texas Stadium and he was the special teams coach that year. The officials were flagging Mike's guys all day long, and Ditka was stomping and cussing and fuming along the sidelines. Finally, the officials told him he had better take it easy or he was gone.

Well, it got to be the fourth quarter and they flagged his team one more time, this time for offsides. Ditka went out onto the field and was real calm, and he said to the official, "Excuse me, sir. Are you a member of the Fellowship of Christian Athletes?"

The official kind of looked at him like, huh? "No," he said. "Then f--k you!" Ditka yelled. Landry just melted on the sidelines. They took Ditka away after that.

CONQUERING THE MOUNTAIN

After the Super Bowl one year a bunch of Cowboys went skiing in Vail, Colorado. There were about eight couples—Ditka, Manders, Reeves, Lee Roy, myself, and our wives among them.

Well, Ditka couldn't ski for shit, but of course that didn't mean anything to him. With him, it was always full-speed ahead, even if you didn't know what you were doing. The rest of us were all pretty good skiers, so we took the chair lift to the top of the mountain and Ditka came right along with us. His wife at the time, Marge, went along, too. She was wearing a purple outfit that must have cost her a couple of grand, at least. She had on purple pants, purple boots, a purple jacket, a purple hat, and a blond wig. She looked sensational!

Well, she came off that chair lift at the top and it was all iced over. She flew right off that mountain and rolled over and over a few times and her blond wig and purple hat flew right off and rolled a couple hundred feet down the mountain.

While the rest of us picked her up, Mike took off. She was really pissed. We were all asking how she was and her husband was off skiing in the other direction. He couldn't have cared less. Hey, he had a job to do. He had to conquer that mountain.

> The first black Chicago Bears quarterback was aptly named Willie Thrower.

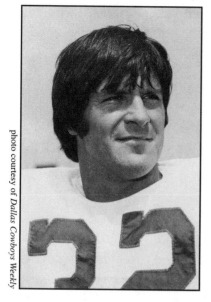

It took Mike about an hour to ski down that hill. He'd ski across and fall. Then he'd get up and cuss awhile, and then he'd ski across and fall and cuss some more. By the time he got down to the bottom, he had fallen so many times his sweater was soaked and it had stretched all the way down to his knees. It looked like a trench coat and he looked like a walrus. He had snot and ice frozen in his mustache and he was sweating like a bull on mating day. This mother was hot!

I figured Mike had to be so miserable when we finally got him down that all he'd want to do would be to go in the lodge and drink. Wrong. Not Ditka. He got down to the bottom of the slope, took one final head-over-ashcan fall, stood up, and said, "Let's go again!"

BAD FOR BUSINESS

Ditka opened a dinner-dance club in Dallas called The Sportspage, and it did unbelievable business. People were lined up on the sidewalk every night begging to get a table. And on Sundays after the game, you couldn't buy your way in. That's where all the players went after the game so it attracted a crowd. People would get to drink and dance and see all their football heroes up close.

That went on for two and a half years. Then all of a sudden Ditka thought he was a restaurant tycoon instead of just a damn good tight end. So he took his profits and opened up a joint in Richardson, Texas, called The Hungry Hunter. They served wild boar, bear meat, quail—stuff like that. Hell, they even had ostrich eggs.

When Mike opened that place he figured he'd retire in two years. But the damn place didn't do any business. How many times do you say to your wife, "Geez, honey, you know what I really feel like tonight? An ostrich egg!"

After that fiasco, Ditka bought some land in Wolf Creek Pass and opened up a ski area. I don't know what Mike thought he knew about skiing, but it wasn't enough. They didn't get any snow the first year and the place bombed.

So, in the end, he blew most of the money he'd made on The Sportspage trying to hit another big one. Before he knew it, he was back at tight end with nothing in the bank and a few good years left in him. Good thing he knew how to coach.

Ditka also owned a bar with Dave Edwards in Houston. I walked in one night and there was Mike.

"How's it going, Mike?" I asked him.

"Well, it's great," Ditka says. "But those Varmint brothers came in last week. I told them to drink what they wanted and they just got drunker than hell. They were slobbering and pinching the girls and pulling their dresses over their heads. I'd have asked them to leave but I didn't know how. Finally, they got ready to go. Then Don got up on the stage with the band and there's slobber coming out of his mouth, and he yells, 'Hey, turn that off. I got something to say.' "

"So they turned the music off and Tolbert screams, 'I'll see all you sonuvabitches later.' "

> At halftime of a New Orleans Saints game in 1968, Charleston Heston drove a chariot and rode an ostrich while filming the movie Number One.

"They finally stumbled out of the place," Ditka said. "Now that's hard on business."

Ditka didn't have much luck with his friends in football. They were the main attraction of the place but they were also big pains. I was there the night E. J. Holub, the behemoth linebacker for the Kansas City Chiefs, came in. Only problem was he came in on a horse. And it wasn't no Shetland pony either. Damn thing looked like a Clydesdale.

We were all in there after the game and we looked up and saw E. J. on his trusty steed. He came right through the front doors of Ditka's place, went down the stairs, backed that baby right up in the corner, and yelled, "Y'all get my horse some beer."

He sat on that horse for an hour just sipping beer and bullshitting. Then he rode on out of there the same way he came in. And there was poor old Ditka in the back of the bar with this sorry look on his face, watching his investment go to hell.

"Ah, geez," he said. "Now that's hard on business."

"TEX" DITKA, AMARILLO SLIM, AND THE VARMINT BROTHERS

DONNIE TOLBERT

photo courtesy of *Dallas Cowboys Weekly*

The Varmint brothers are legendary in NFL circles and to anyone who was connected with the league in the 1960s and early 1970s. Donnie, Diron, Paul, and Charlie Tolbert are from the University of Texas in Richmond. Diron spent most of his career with the LA Rams and the Washington Redskins, while Donnie spent the majority of his career with the Dallas Cowboys. They spent many a memorable occasion with Mike Ditka. Although they have calmed down in recent years and are now respectable businessmen, they still cut a wide swathe in the NFL.

Doff Briscoe (now the ex-governor of Texas) was running for governor, and Dan Reeves and Walt Garrison were riding the wagon of a guy named Ben Barnes, who at that time was the lieutenant governor of Texas. So a guy named Lee Roy Caffey, who played for the Cowboys, said, "Hey, let's get some guys and back Briscoe." Briscoe flew into Dallas, and we went up and met him to have dinner and a few drinks. Then we all went out to Texas Instruments and shook hands with everybody coming onto the line in the morning. We made a few stops and he was really appreciative. He was running about third in the ranking.

About two weeks later, they caught Ben Barnes in a bank scandal. Our man Briscoe went straight to the top. He won the nomination and won as governor of Texas. He said to us, "I want to take you guys on a big hunt."

So we got all our guys together and drove from Austin out to San Antonio airport. We were picking up Dave Edwards, Craig Morton, and Mike Ditka. They had all worked for Briscoe. We got to the airport and said, "Where the hell is Ditka? That son of a bitch didn't even show up." Then Ditka stepped out from behind a column where he had been hiding and said, "I knew I was in trouble when I saw all them damn Boone's Farm bottles come flying out of the car."

We got down to the ranch, rode around, hunted, and had a big time, and that night they got into a poker game. A bunch of judges were there, and Doff had also invited all his bankers and everyone on his board of directors. We all had dinner, had a few drinks, and carried on. Then they decided to play poker. A bunch of them wanted to play, and they weren't playing penny ante—they were playing pot limit. Ditka sat down next to a judge and got on him because the judge had all the damn chips. Ditka said, "You little son of a bitch, call or get out of the game."

He had a case of twelve-year-old St. James scotch. They were all raising hell. They were playing high-low split and had a two-pot game. The judge still had all the chips. Ditka said, "Deal the damn

> In 1961, Alabama assistant football coach Howard Schnellenberger personally picked up Joe Namath in Beaver Falls, Pennsylvania, and drove him to the Alabama campus in Tuscaloosa.

cards. You run a kangaroo court down there in Commerce, I know you do."

They were raising hell, so one of Doff's guys came over and said, "Any of you all want to go out and shoot a mountain lion?" So four or five of us went with him. On the way out there we caught a small jackrabbit. We brought it back to the house with us.

When we got back, they were still playing cards, and Ditka was still on the judge. He was saying the same things: "You little sawed-off son of a bitch, running a kangaroo court, deal the cards." The judge had all these

It was way more cursing than God likes to hear from a football person during peacetime.

cards, and he said, "What was the name of that little game we were playing? How do you play this game, little fellers?" And Ditka said, "You got all the chips and you're asking what kind of a game we're playing?"

I said, "Look at Ditka. He's in there raising hell, just tearing everybody every way. Let's get the rabbit and put it in Ditka's bed." So I went outside and got the rabbit.

Ditka, Dave Edwards, my brother Diron Tolbert, and my old roommate Eddie Padgett were in the Sam Rayburn suite. This wasn't a camp house—this was plush. The Sam Rayburn suite was beautiful and immaculate—the beds were made and it had a big sleeping porch. There were about twelve to fifteen of us, and we all loudly crept into the suite. Dave Edwards said, "What are you all doing?"

We asked him which bed was Ditka's. Then we took the rabbit and put it between Ditka's pillows.

Ditka came in at about 2:00 in the morning. He pulled the covers back and laid his head down, right on the rabbit. You could have heard him holler all the way to Mexico City; it was hilarious. He was after us all the next day. He said, "You all have had it." It was way more cursing than God likes to hear from a football person during peacetime.

When he got up the next day, he and the judge were the best of friends. They were inseparable; they rode all over the ranch, hugging each other and telling each other what buddies they were. And just the night before they were killing each other.

> Q: What comic strip characters are named after sports figures?
>
> A: The B. C. character in "Doonesbury" is named after former Yale and Cleveland Browns quarterback Brian Dowling. The title character in the current sports comic strip "Gil Thorp" is named for Gil Hodges and Jim Thorpe.

photo courtesy of *Dallas Cowboys Weekly*

NO AD-LIBBING
THOMAS "HOLLYWOOD" HENDERSON

Hollywood Henderson was a controversial linebacker for the Cowboys in the 1970s. Drafted in a low round out of Langston University in Oklahoma, a virtually unknown school for football, Henderson soon made a mark on the Cowboys scene with his running talents.

T**he Cowboys' opponent in Super Bowl X in 1976 was the Pittsburgh Steelers, a powerful defensive team that was back for its second year in a row. Pittsburgh had defeated Minnesota by a score of 16–6 in Super Bowl IX, in which the Steelers held Fran Tarkenton to six points, a testament to their defense's quickness. "Mean" Joe Greene, Ernie Holmes, Dwight**

Dwight White, and L. C. Greenwood were a formidable front line, and middle linebacker Jack Lambert was a wild man in the mold of Dick Butkus.

On the urging of special teams coach Mike Ditka, the Cowboys' game plan began with a surprise. Though Thomas Henderson was a linebacker, he could run the 40 in 4.5. Against the Cardinals on a reverse he had run a kickoff back ninety-seven yards for a touchdown, and before the game Ditka explained to the rookie that he was to do it again. For one of the few times in his life, Thomas Henderson had butterflies.

The coach I had the best relationship with that first year was Mike Ditka.

Let me tell you how I was feeling before that game. Here's a guy who had witnessed his mother shoot his stepfather with a gun nine years before, whose best friend had been shot at close range and killed six years before, and who had graduated from Langston University just one year before. I had played one season in the NFL and had run for a touchdown. But to be in the Super Bowl—that was a different story.

Before the game, I had already wrapped myself up. I had on the elbow pads, the hand pads, and all this extra padding, because I was going to kick butt on those special teams. Then, after we warmed up, Ditka came over to me and said, "If we win the toss, we're going with the reverse." So I had to take all that padding off. I had to put stickum on. It scared me to death! I was like, "You're going to let me handle the ball the first play of the Super Bowl?"

There have been times in my life when I've been afraid, but this was the first stage fright I have ever had. It was all that pressure. Coach Landry was very concerned that a linebacker was handling the ball. He liked the results, but he was always nervous about a linebacker handling the ball, which is a legitimate concern. I agreed with Landry at that moment: "I'm a linebacker. Give the ball to somebody else." But on the other hand, I was like, "Give me the ball. Let's go." I was a running back in high school, in my early days; I knew how to run.

Ditka was a very intense man. All he wanted you to do was do your job and do it right.

They kicked it off, I faked my little deal, Preston Pearson took it deep, and I had to go around. I was standing on the thirty-yard line, and I had to go back to him at about the ten. He started my way and I went his way. He gave the ball to me, and I took it the other way, and a wall set up. When I turned the corner, everything looked pretty good, except the Steelers weren't quite as fooled as the Cardinals had been a few weeks earlier. At some point, I thought I could have cut back.

But instead I ran the play the way it was designed. I didn't freelance and try to make something happen. Ditka liked that. He didn't like you to go out there and start doing your own tap dance. "No ad-libbing, goddamn it," he'd say.

The coach I had the best relationship with that first year was Mike Ditka. He was an offensive coach and a special teams coach. He liked the way I got things done. To this day, Ditka will say, "Thomas Henderson was a good football player. He's crazy as hell, but he's a good football player." He'll say that because all the coaches who ever coached me never saw me back down. You'll watch films on a player and he'll get hurt and wince and run or dodge. They never saw me back down. I don't have that in me.

Ditka was a very intense man. All he wanted you to do was do your job and do it right. He would tell me to go down the field and do this or that, and I did it. And he never saw me back down.

I remember playing one of my finest games in Super Bowl XII in 1978. Ditka, the consummate competitor, said to me, "Thomas," —and he knew I loved doing shit like this—"on the first punt, if you get a shot at Rick Upchurch, take the penalty. Just take him out. Don't hurt him, but get his attention. Make sure he's going to be looking for you the rest of the day." We were all afraid of Rick Upchurch. We felt that he could beat us returning kickoffs and punts.

I flew down the field with my mission orders, and I took a fifteen-yard penalty. I just creamed Upchurch. I came over to the sideline, and Ditka had moved away, so I had to see Landry. I said to him, "Well, Ditka told me to do that." Landry turned to look for Ditka and he couldn't even find him!

> The oldest NFL record belongs to George Halas. He made the longest fumble return for a touchdown (ninety-seven yards) in 1923.

THE MONSTER OF THE MIDWAY
JIM McMAHON

Jim McMahon, a graduate of Brigham Young, was a first-round draft pick for the Chicago Bears in 1982. He played with the Bears for seven years, and led the team to their 1985 Super Bowl win. McMahon retired in 1996.

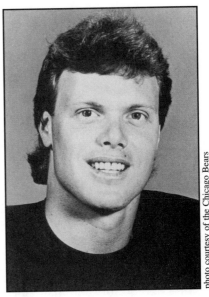

photo courtesy of the Chicago Bears

For many years, American Airlines hosted an annual golf outing featuring their best corporate customers playing with famous athletes. The tournament rotated among the top golf resorts in North America. In February 1986, the tournament paid its third visit to Scottsdale, Arizona. It was less than a month after the Bears won the Super Bowl. Of all the famous athletes playing, Jim McMahon was easily the most in demand.

The final day of the tournament was one of the worst ever weather-wise. It was cold, windy, and rainy. If ever an athlete could beg off signing autographs without an explanation, that was the day. When McMahon came off the eighteenth green, every fan still braving the elements was waiting for him. He stood there for almost an hour signing autographs and posing for pictures. Someone asked him what Scottsdale bar he was going to that evening. He looked up from his signing and replied, "I'm going to the best bar in the world tonight—my mother-in-law's house in San Francisco."

Before I went up to my first Bears camp in Platteville, Wisconsin, I didn't know anything at all about Mike Ditka. All I knew of the Bears was Brian Piccolo, Gale Sayers, and Dick Butkus. I grew up in the Bay area, so I was a Raiders/49ers fan; those were my teams.

I liked Ditka's attitude. I liked the fact that his number one priority was to win. That's why you play sports and that's why you compete—to win. Every player wants to do his best, but hell, it's no fun unless you win.

Ditka and I would have a run-in every week. Our goals were the same; he just had a different opinion on how to achieve those goals. When I was on the field, I felt that was my job. I felt like, I know what the hell I'm doing—just leave me alone. He wanted to call all the plays and do this and that. But I was taught in college that if you see something to exploit, exploit it. Since we didn't throw the ball a lot, if I got a chance to change the play to a pass, I would do it. We'd scream and yell at each other, because his natural tendency was to blow up if something didn't work. Then we'd watch the film and he'd say, "Well, now I see why you did what you did." I think he eventually just figured out that I knew what the hell I was doing. That's why the guys playing now are struggling. If the headsets go out, they can't call a play. They're so reliant on their coaches to spoon-feed them everything. Hell, I don't know what they learn in college anymore.

I told Mike many times I wished I had played with him. He played the game the way it's supposed to be played. He didn't think I studied enough. I told him if he'd ever been in the huddle with me, he'd have a different opinion. I said to him, "You know, you don't have to be a rocket scientist to run this offense. You could be brain-dead almost." The offense didn't change in the seven years I was there.

O. J. Simpson's cousin is Ernie Banks. Their grandfathers were twin brothers.

I didn't socialize with Mike, but I played a lot of golf with his wife, Diana. She would always say, "Mike likes you a lot." I'd say, "Then why is he cussing me out every Sunday?" I used to play with her and her friends all the time; she was great. His regular game was cards. I heard a lot of stories about him throwing chairs and card tables through the wall, just because he wanted to win. He hates losing. I hate losing as much as him. Any game Ditka plays—air hockey, pool, golf—he wants to win. That's where you separate the men from the boys. If you're going to do something, be the best at it. You have to have it inside you to win. You've got to have that something inside you that says you're not going to lose that game.

> **I liked Ditka's attitude. I liked the fact that his number one priority was to win.**

In '85, I watched from the sidelines as the Minnesota game slipped away. You could see it in the guys' faces when they came off the field. I was yelling at Mike to let me in. I had been in traction on the Monday and Tuesday before the game. I got out of the hospital Wednesday morning, went to practice that afternoon, and then flew up to Minnesota Thursday morning for the Thursday night game. Not only were my back and neck screwed up, I also had an infected turf burn on my leg. My damn calf was twice as big as my thigh.

On my very first play he called a screen pass, and I didn't throw the screen. I stumbled away from the center, I was so wobbly. I knew it was a blitz, which is man-to-man coverage, and a screen is not very good against that unless you use a technique we called "the spy." I happened to look downfield and saw Willie Gault running his guy off like he was supposed to on a screen. He was ten yards past his man, so I just threw it to him. Mike was yelling at me as I came off the field, "Damn it, what play did you call?" I told him I had called screen pass he gave me. He said, "Why'd you throw it to Willie?" I said, "Because he was open. We scored, what are you mad about?" I think he thought I did everything just to piss him off, but I did it to amuse myself. Sitting in those meetings a couple of hours a day bored me. I'm a player; I just want to play. I didn't practice a whole lot in my career, and it didn't seem to hurt me.

PERSONALITY CONFLICTS

Ditka and I have had our moments, and we probably always will. He said I did certain things for the sole purpose of aggravating him, but I really didn't. I didn't wake up every morning wondering, "How can I annoy Ditka today?" It's hard enough just to wake up in the morning, let alone think and plot.

> **I told Mike many times I wished I had played with him.**

I was hurt one season, and we didn't talk for a few weeks. We never exchanged a civil word. Jerry Vainisi even called me up to his office one day after practice, sat me down, and told me I had to resolve my personality conflict with Mike. Personality conflict? What personality conflict? I was injured. I wasn't playing. There was no reason for him to talk to me, or for me to talk to him.

Besides, Ditka did talk to me, as he pointed out when someone asked him about the situation. He came over to me on the sidelines in Dallas and screamed, "Shut the f--k up, McMahon!" That's talking, isn't it? And I know it was Mike, because his veins were sticking out of his neck and his face was red as a beet, like it was ready to explode. That had to be my good friend Sybil, the one who wears a necktie on the sidelines, the one we all figured would strangle himself someday with that same necktie. He'll get mad and he'll reach to make that knot tighter, and by the time the paramedics get to him with the oxygen it'll be too late.

I remember clearly why he screamed at me in Dallas. That was the game in which we humiliated the Cowboys 44–0. Steve Fuller started for us at quarterback, and he did a great job. Our defense was awesome, as usual. I was yelling from the bench for our guys to really give it to the Dallas quarterback, Danny White, which they eventually did.

"Shut the f--k up, McMahon!" Ditka roared. "What's the problem, Mike?" I asked. "They get Danny White hurt, and they'll put in (Gary) Hogeboom, and he's better than White," Ditka said. "So shut up."

I just walked away from him. That was the same day he got mad at me because of the way I was dressed. I had on a normal shirt and faded blue jeans. He got mad because he thought I didn't look presentable. Hell, I had on a pair of ostrich boots that were worth more than his entire wardrobe. Mike doesn't worry about the unimportant things. Most of the time, anyway.

We had another episode later in the season at Giants Stadium when we played the New York Jets. I called an audible and Walter Payton just got smashed on the play, sort of like when I screwed up early in the Super Bowl. When I got back to the sidelines, I could see that Mike wasn't in the best of moods. I don't know how I was able to make that deduction. Maybe it was the fact that, with sixty thousand people screaming in the arena, Mike's voice was the only one anybody heard.

> In 1999, Monday Night Football became the longest-running prime-time entertainment series ever, breaking a tie with Walt Disney at twenty-nine years.

photo courtesy of the Chicago Bears

"You motherf--ker," he yelled at me. "F--k you," I said.

The national TV cameras recorded our little conversation. That was a Saturday in December. The next day, when a lot of pro football games were being played, the people from CBS asked me to stay over in New York to appear on the NFL Today show.

Naturally, they had those film clips ready, and naturally, they asked me about the incident.

"Well," I said, "that about sums up our relationship." I never lie, particularly on Sundays.

But Mike has mellowed since we both came to the Bears in 1982. He was really uptight when he started as coach. One of the worst things he did was get all over guys for making mistakes. He'd take them out of games, scream at them in public, and go crazy on the sidelines. It got so bad that the players couldn't relax, because they were afraid of what Ditka might do if they dropped a pass or missed an assignment. He could really get out of control, and so badly that he'd lose his grasp on the game itself. He was the Monster of the Midway.

Ditka was just as hard on himself. We heard stories about some of the wild things he did as an assistant with the Cowboys before he left Dallas for Chicago. He could throw a pretty mean clipboard, we were told. He could throw a pretty good fit, too. Mike Ditka had a major-league temper.

We found that out after our fourth game of the 1983 season, which we lost in overtime to Baltimore, 22–19. Ditka came into the locker room and started pounding on an equipment locker. All of a sudden, he looked up at the trainer and said, "I think I broke my hand." He had. We didn't know whether to laugh or cry.

SPECIAL WINE

During the last couple of years we were together, Ditka wasn't quite as high-strung, and that helped the players play better. The fact that we were 18–1 probably helped us get away with things we never would have gotten away with otherwise, but the point is that Ditka was most concerned with how we played on Sunday. He didn't bug us about some of the nutty things we said or did.

Of course, he said and did some pretty strange things himself. There was that sixth game of 1985, when we whipped the 49ers in San Francisco 26–10. That win not only kept us unbeaten at 6–0, it repaid the 49ers for knocking us out of the playoffs the year before. Mike really wanted to win that game. He told us that if we won, he'd share some of his special wine on the long flight back to Chicago that night.

Well, we never got to taste any of that wine. Later, we found out why. Mike had tasted all of the wine himself. He was smashed, hammered, bobbing, and weaving. There's no way he should have been allowed to drive home that night. Vainisi felt the same way and offered him a lift. Apparently, the police felt the same way, too.

Five minutes after we left O'Hare Airport, Ditka was pulled over for drunk driving. He had said something on TV after the game about how he might celebrate a little on the plane, to the point where he might not be able to see when he got back home. Evidently, the Illinois State Police were watching.

A few of us took the same highway home, and he damn near ran over a couple of guys. He was all over the road. He would have killed himself if he hadn't have been stopped by the cops. When we caught up to where he'd been nailed, we saw his car and the police car on the side of the road. Nobody pulled over. We just honked our horns and drove on by. I guess his wife, Diana, had to come and get him.

The next morning, I heard about it on the radio on the way to Halas Hall. So had most of the other guys. Naturally, it was a hot topic in the locker room, and when Mike held his meeting, he didn't look too good. He looked like a coach who hadn't lost a game, but had lost his license for a few months.

"Fellas . . . I did something very stupid last night," he said. There were a few of us in the room coughing loudly to keep from cracking up. That must have been real special wine indeed.

Ironically, this guy who could pound the streets at night with the best of them later told my roommate, Kurt Becker, and me to watch ourselves. I had a bad first half in Tampa one year, and he came over

> The NFL since 1968 has given every player the Wonderlic test (a human resources test measuring the ability to acquire and use job knowledge). In a recent year, 118,549 non-NFL people took the test and only 4 had a perfect score of 50. In thirty years, the only NFL player with a perfect score was Pat McInally of Harvard in 1968. McInally starred with the Cincinnati Bengals as tight end and punter.

to me and said, "That's what you get for staying out all night." I hadn't been out all night, or even half the night, but that was Mike.

Ditka also warned Becker that alcohol and football don't mix. He told Becker that he would fine us one week's paycheck if we were caught breaking curfew, and that management might have to put a cage around our room on the road just to keep us in at night. This from a coach who got picked up by the police for driving under the influence! That never happened to me. Besides, I don't mix my alcohol with football. I don't mix my alcohol with anything. I prefer beer. It's much better for you than wine.

I'm not saying Mike is a hypocrite, he just does some weird things. He's a born-again Christian who says he's very religious, which is fine. But I guess for three hours every Sunday that doesn't hold, because I wouldn't even use some of the words that come out of his mouth when he's coaching. I've never even heard some of those words!

FINDING OURSELVES

Mike Ditka just wants to win. He wants to win more than anything.

Every so often, he'd give us that same line: "If you forty-five guys don't want to play, we'll go out and get forty-five guys who do." That was part of his "prima donna" speech. When you hear that twice a week, it tends to get old. Mike has to get some new material.

Still, he was great at keeping his players levelheaded. He had to have known that the 1985 Bears didn't have a whole lot of attitude problems. Just like he had to have known that we weren't a bunch of prima donnas. We worked our butts off, and he knew it. But whether he wanted us to know he knew is another matter. He was forever reviewing films of Sunday victories on Monday and knocking us down to size.

For instance, we finished one regular season in Detroit. We beat the Lions 37–17 to finish 15–1. It wasn't a great performance, and we realized that, but it got the job done. After the game, Ditka told us we were full of horsefeathers and that we had no chance in the playoffs if we continued to play that way. We had just won a game on the road by twenty points to go 15–1, and he was giving us grief.

> **I never looked at Ditka, but I don't imagine he found anything funny in my sick and sarcastic humor.**

"You've got a couple days off for Christmas, fellas," he said. "I hope you go home and find yourselves."

On the flight home that night—it was a short one, so we didn't have any special wine on board—I slipped up front and grabbed hold of the public-address system. I told the guys we were about to land and that they should have a happy holiday, but that above all, they should try to find themselves. When I walked to the back of the plane, the guys were roaring. I never looked at Ditka, but I don't imagine he found anything funny in my sick and sarcastic humor.

I do think, though, that deep down Ditka respects a guy who will stand up for what he believes in. He might even like me for that, in some strange way, because that's the way he is. Mike doesn't watch every word he says. He's not afraid to say something that's going to motivate the next week's opponent, because he knows next week's game is going to be won on the field, not in the newspapers. It's you against us, baby. Let's see who's better. Let's see who's stronger. That's the way Mike operates. That's the way I think.

Considering his background as a bona fide free spirit, I don't think

Mike expected us all to be the same, on the field or off. He knows that you can't lock forty-five guys in their rooms at 8:00 the night before a game. Some guys will stay in, which is fine. I couldn't. For one thing, I couldn't sleep that well or that long before a game. I liked to go out and have a few beverages and relax. Sometimes I forgot to check the clock, but it's ridiculous to be knocking on the doors of grown men to make sure they haven't broken curfew. Fortunately, Mike wasn't into that. Every once in a while he'd give you a little message, to let you know that he was watching. But when you win like we won, a good coach is going to let a lot slide.

Is Mike Ditka a good coach? Well, he knows the game, but he gets a little wrapped up in his innovations sometimes. That's surprising, I know, because he is a basic guy, no frills. But Mike did spend a lot of time in Dallas under Tom Landry, the head coach of the Cowboys, and he got caught up with movement and all those different formations. That's great stuff, if you know what you're doing. The thing is, the more complex you make the game, the more chances you have to make mistakes. If it were up to me, football would be as simple as possible. Mike is that way, deep down, but every once in a while, when he puts his thinking cap on, you never know quite what to expect.

He can be very stubborn, too. I've talked to his assistant coaches, and they say he's a good guy to work for. He listens, he can have some fun, and he doesn't demand that you spend twenty-four hours a day on the job, looking at films and all that, even though he is in his office at 5:00 A.M. during the season. I don't know when he sees his family. His assistants also say that Mike's pretty good at taking a game plan that's been carefully drawn up by the staff, then changing it all around to do it his way.

Maybe he is a genius in a way. Not with the X's and O's, but in getting players to be committed to win. When I first got to the Bears, the attitude wasn't very good. He said there were too many guys around whose highlight of the week wasn't game day, but payday. You don't want to pay the price, he said, you're just putting in time and going through the motions.

I'll give Ditka full credit for getting rid of those players. He let them know that he wanted no part of them, and he gave them a chance to do it his way. When they didn't, they were gone. That's what got that ball rolling—the selection of the right forty-five guys. Mike was right when he said that some of our so-called second- or third-stringers might not have had the ability that other players on teams that didn't win the Super Bowl had. But our guys were perfect for us; they fit in just right.

Mike, as committed as he is to God, doesn't believe it's God's will when you lose a game. We had a few players who would pray in the shower room, all by themselves. These were the same guys who would drop a pass and say, "Well, He meant it that way." Well, I believe in God, and I believe that God's will is that everybody tries his hardest, everybody tries to succeed, and everybody tries to win. You can use God as an inspiration, but not as a crutch.

That was just one of the factions, or cliques, that used to hurt the Bears. When you have a few guys going off by themselves to pray before a game, it sort of sets them apart. A lot of people would have trouble believing this, but I said a little prayer to God before every game, too. I asked him to help me do my best and to help me stay healthy for my family's sake. But I didn't run off and pray away from my teammates. And if I played a lousy game, I didn't say it

> In football pileups, Walter Payton used to lay at the bottom and untie his opponents' shoelaces. That's why a lot of defenders put tape over their laces today.

was the Lord's will.

I'm partial, of course. I think if you have forty-five beer-drinking fools who love each other, you have a good chance of having a good football team. Judging by some of the things Mike's done as a coach, I have to think he partly agrees. After Ditka came, we didn't have the divisions in the team we used to have. We didn't have the offense on one side of the room and the

They say that there's a lot of Mike Ditka in me, and a lot of me in Mike Ditka.

defense on another side, blaming each other. We were all together, and Ditka was a big reason for that. He kept stressing that you can't be pointing fingers, that it's not the offensive team or the defensive team that matters. It's the team, period. The Bears.

Ditka could get under your skin at times, that's for sure. He'd get you furious enough at him that you'd go out and knock a guy's block off, just to get him off your back, just to prove him wrong. Ditka was pretty smart that way. He kept pushing and pushing until you were right at the edge. But he also knew when to lift you up. He's a man's man, when you get right down to it.

As serious as he is, Mike can make you laugh. He could make some really strong pregame speeches, but he could also go the other way. The Saturday night before the Super Bowl, he showed up for our meeting and it was obvious he wasn't going to give us the "Win one for the Gipper" business. Instead, he started imitating some of the bizarre things that had taken place that week, especially those things involving me.

He wore sunglasses, he brought up the headbands and the acupuncture, and then he turned around and dropped his pants right in our faces. That was his way of toasting my sore behind, I suppose. That was also his way of mimicking what I'd done earlier that week, when a helicopter flew over our secret practice session. I flipped them a moon, just to show everybody where I hurt. Mike was just trying to act as demented as me. It worked. It was pretty funny.

They say there's a lot of Mike Ditka in me, and a lot of me in Mike Ditka. That might be true. Some of the things he did made me mad and some of the things I did made him mad. But we both wanted to do the same thing: win and let the rest take care of itself. I'd still call him if I was in trouble or if I needed help. I'd want him on my side in a fight. And, if we were teammates, I'm sure we'd go out for a few beers—unless, of course, he wanted to drink wine. In that case, I'd make sure to drive him home.

One of the things about Ditka, who was a mean and rough tight end for the Bears when they won the NFL title in 1963, is that he was a hell-raiser as a player. There's this story about George Halas showing films one day when he was still the coach. He was pointing out some things about the next opponent—strengths, weaknesses, that sort of thing. All of a sudden, Mike stood up in the back of the room and yelled at the top of his lungs, "F--k 'em!" I don't know if the story is true, but it sure sounds like Ditka.

So does that anecdote about how Ditka was fighting with Halas, trying to get a raise. Ditka got angry and frustrated and said, "The old man throws quarters around like manhole covers." Way to go, Mike! That's what I mean when I say Ditka probably would have been a great guy to have as a teammate, a lot more fun that he was to have as a coach. We would have probably been out drinking every night. I know he would have been out every night. I know I would have been out every night. It only stands to reason that we would have gone out together every night.

SEPARATING THE MEN FROM THE BOYS
MIKE SINGLETARY

Mike Singletary exploded onto the Chicago sports scene in 1981 as the Bears' first-round draft pick from Baylor University. He quickly established himself among the very top Bears players of all time with his savage play and wide-eyed intensity.

photo courtesy of the Chicago Bears

I'll never forget the first day I saw Ditka. Intensity oozed from his pores. That first day, you knew change was ahead. But for good or for bad, no one was quite sure. He instructed Ted Plumb, our receivers coach, to call roll. *Roll.* "Well, fellas," Ditka said, calling us together for the first time, "we have only forty-nine players, and we're going to get out here, and we're going to see who's best. We're going to separate the men from the boys around here, and see who wants to work and who doesn't. If you don't want to win, if you don't want to sacrifice, then you don't want to be here."

Even if you did want to "be here," there were times when you didn't. He had two mini-camps, and one was in Scottsdale, Arizona. It was ninety degrees in the shade, and the training regimen was more Green Beret than Bear. Forty-yard dashes until we dropped. Run here. Sprint there. Miles and miles before we slept. The mumbling and grumbling would have been louder if anyone had had enough strength to speak. "I want football players," he said time and time

photo courtesy of the Chicago Bears

again. "Too many guys around here have too many things going on outside of football."

It boiled down to one word: pride. Pride in yourself. Pride in your teammates. Pride in your commitment to improve. "I'm proudest of being a Bear," he would say. Ditka! It even sounded tough. From that first day, I never doubted his ability to unify and push his team in a positive direction.

His golden rule was that you played by his. He never begged us to do anything. If he said the meeting was at 9:00 A.M., he didn't mean 8:59 or 9:01. You did things a certain way—his way—or you were cut. Yet, at the same time that he was filling the waiver wires, you sensed that he would accept deviation, a free spirit or two. And even though the papers were already calling Halas's hiring of him "madness" and knocking Ditka's intelligence, Ditka was going about his business, building a bond between offense and defense that never before existed.

"You don't win games with defense," he said. "It takes offense, special teams. We're not going to win until everyone does his job, because winning and losing depends on all three." He didn't care whom we played. "They're playing the Bears! The Bears!" There was nothing phony about him. You'd see him in his office at 5:30 A.M., jogging the halls, then again at midnight, turning off the lights. He wanted to be the best. That's all I knew about him. We rarely talked—only once or twice a season in depth—but I knew all I needed to know, or wanted to know. He wanted to be the best. That was good enough for me.

But the transition wasn't easy. He cleaned house for one year. In a way, he reminded me of a tailor, because whenever someone wasn't putting out or was getting too big for his britches, Ditka would always be there to cut him down to size. If he sensed a certain swagger seeping into your step, or a head beginning to swell, he always reached for the scissors. Chop, chop. "Hey, just look at it this way," he'd say. "You could be working for a living. And really, what can you do? I don't think half of you are smart enough to get a job. We don't need you. If you want to leave and get a better deal, fine. Leave."

I'll never forget the first day I saw Ditka. Intensity oozed from his pores.

In the strike-shortened season of 1982, we went 3–6, and the press was screaming for Ditka's scalp. McMahon was hot and cold, still learning the offense, and we were still a year away from a blockbuster draft.

Halas had died in October 1982, at the age of eighty-eight, and was replaced by Bears president Mike McCaskey, a Yale graduate, ex-Peace Corps volunteer, Harvard professor, and author of a book on management. Despite the eighteen months remaining on his three-year contract, Ditka wasn't sure where he stood with McCaskey, a man with a corporate outlook on life who was in the process of restructuring our front office, paying particular attention to improving our scouting department. We had only two scouts for fifty states, the smallest such department in the league. McCaskey was fully aware that only one pick past the fourth round had ever made our club between 1978 and 1982.

The changes paid off in 1983. Big-time talent arrived in the form of Jimbo Covert, Willie Gault, Mike Richardson, Dave Duerson, Pat Dunsmore, Richard Dent, and Mark Bortz. I had made All-Pro my second season, and had signed a six-year, $1.6-million deal with the Bears, much of the money deferred. The contract had been negotiated by Tom Williams, my friend in Houston. "Treat me fair," I said. "I want to die a Bear." My only stipulation: if at any time this contract becomes unfair, we'll work together to bring it up to date.

Except for my rookie year in 1981, Mike was the only head coach I ever had in the pros.

Q: Pat Summerall's real first name is George. Why is he called Pat?
A: Because when he was a kicker with the New York Giants football team, the newspapers would always print: "P.A.T. Summerall." P.A.T. stood for "Point After Touchdown."

MIKE DITKA ON DUANE THOMAS

photo courtesy of *Dallas Cowboys Weekly*

Duane Thomas was a big factor in us winning. He was a good football player. He was a good all-around receiver, runner, and blocker. He was a fluid runner who never took a real hard hit. He was like Jim Brown. He knew how to give and go, slip and slide—all that stuff. He was an excellent blocker, which people didn't know. Dan Reeves worked with him and said, "That guy is really smart." He knew the fullback and halfback spots. He had to know both because Walt Garrison got hurt and Duane had to go to fullback with Calvin Hill at halfback.

But it was just uncomfortable and no fun to be around him. Once we were playing the Giants in Yankee Stadium. I always made a habit of going up and wishing everybody good luck before a game. I went up to Duane and just patted him on the back and said, "Good luck." He didn't acknowledge it. I went on my way. We played the game. The following Tuesday, I was sitting beside my locker reading the paper in Dallas before practice and he came up to me and said, "Hey, man, don't ever hit me on the back before a game. It breaks my concentration."

I said, "Hey, Duane, go f--k yourself."

That was our conversation.

Chapter 3

photo courtesy of *Dallas Cowboys Weekly*

Dave McGinnis

Rick Jago

Tom Hurvis

Mac Chuchill

Kyle Petty

Jim Rittenberg

Bob Costas

Buddy Diliberto

Mike North

Skip Bayless

Greg Aiello

Vince Tobin

Colleagues

A CLASS ACT
DAVE McGINNIS

photo courtesy of the Arizona Cardinals

Dave McGinnis grew up in the west Texas town of Snyder and starred at TCU. He is one of the few people ever to turn down a head coaching job in the NFL, despite never having held one previously. The Chicago Bears' Mike McCaskey brought the offer to replace Dave Wannstedt to McGinnis in early 1999. McGinnis said thanks but no thanks. He is now a defensive coordinator with the Arizona Cardinals.

Turning down the head coaching job with the Bears in early 1999 was an easy decision to make. I wanted that job so badly, but it was an easy decision to make because everything that is supposed to be there for something to be right was absent. Ditka was one of the first guys to call me, because I had talked to him extensively when I had been up there to interview. He said, "Kid, you're one in a thousand who would have turned it down. If I could right now, I'd come through this phone and kiss you right on the mouth."

It was just incredible, and not only for the people in Chicago. I've still got stacks of mail from executives and assistant coaches in the league who knew what was going wrong. It just points out that there is no right way to do the wrong thing. Something was wrong at the very beginning.

It was extremely, extremely hard to turn it down, believe me. But I knew taking it wasn't right. As I said in my exit interview at O'Hare, I wasn't angry; I was very sad. I was extremely sad that it was handled the way it was. You grow up with principles and things that you know are right, and you can't compromise those for power, and that's what I told Michael. If I compromise my vows for the power, the position, and the money, when I get up in front of this team I'm nobody. When I get up in front of this city, I'm nobody. Because I'm here for a reason: because you respect what I stand for. This is not what I stand for—all of the bluster and everything that goes on. It's like Ditka; people don't know that Mike is very, very religious and spiritual. He'll deal with you—look you straight in the eye and deal with you—from the heart.

> **"If I could right now, I'd come through this phone and kiss you right on the mouth."**

I said to the Bears, "Regardless of how much money you put on this table now, bypass me, because you've lost what is important." That's exactly the way I felt. It's very important to get those positions, but it's more important to take them and be able to be an example when you've got them. If you're in that kind of position, you need to have some influence, and the influence has to be positive. If you can't be positive, you take the position in an underhanded manner—just because of the money.

Ever since the Chicago thing, I've been doing some head-hunting. It's incredible, the response I've received from what happened in Chicago. It helps me to know that some people, especially some owners in this league, do realize how important it is, especially in this climate, to have someone the players can look up to and know is honest.

If you've lived the right way and continue to do the right thing, it will come out and show itself, because there is no right way to do the wrong thing. That other stuff is very temporal and it can't last forever.

It was really a shock when we all got canned in Chicago in '93. I really didn't believe it was going to happen, just because of all that Ditka had done. And like anything else, you run through cycles in this league, so I don't know about all the maneuverings behind the scenes. But we didn't expect it, and when it came, it came as a shock and was very sad.

Just to see the way he handled that—with dignity and confidence and very real emotion. He cried. Because Mike Ditka's a very real guy.

He loved the Bears, and he's a tough guy who's not afraid to cry and show you his emotions. That's another thing that endeared him to the team. Some of the greatest times with him were on those Saturday nights before the ballgames. He would get up with impassioned speeches the guys knew weren't contrived, especially when we were getting ready to play the Packers. During those years, you could feel and see Halas and Lombardi coming out of him. As a coach getting ready to play a ballgame, you were sitting on edge. But even as a fan of the game, you could feel the history coming out of every pore of Ditka's body when he was talking about the game and what it meant. I think that's what

Q: Name three players who quit baseball to star in the NFL and to whom George Steinbrenner gave $100,000 in Yankee bonuses.

A: John Elway, Deion Sanders, and Billy Cannon Jr.

He loved the Bears, and he's a tough guy who's not afraid to cry and show you his emotions.

made him so successful, when he can get a group of men to be as passionate as he is. And that's what he tries to do wherever he is.

We were all at the office when the other shoe fell. We went to the press conference and it was a very emotional, very traumatic time, as it was again in the days afterward, when he gathered us all together. Then he brought us each in individually to talk to us. He told me, "I'll do anything I can to help you. You've been loyal to me, and believe me, from now on, I'll always help you and you can always count on me. And don't worry about me. I'll be fine." It was such a class act.

PEAK PERFORMERS
RICK JAGO

Rick Jago is the marketing director for Old World Industries, which makes Peak Performance Antifreeze.

photo courtesy of Rick Jago

The whole theme was being a "Peak Performer." These guys (Ditka, Petty, and Gretzky) were peak performers. The campaign was really quite well done and I give a lot of credit to the guys who did it. It lasted for about four years. We were all under contract for three years; I think Kyle did it a little longer because he carried the Peak Banner for quite a long time on his car. We then went into sponsoring actual races in Dover, Delaware, under the Peak name, and then we launched the Spitfire brand of spark plugs.

I came in and took over sports marketing as a marketing manager, so I worked with Kyle, Gretzky, and Ditka. Ditka was quite an individual. One time we had to do a deal with him in Chicago, and he was going to speak to the automotive industry on our behalf. Their meeting was at McCormick Place. The entire automotive industry was there for their after-market show. I met him there. He was kind of hacked off because he never does anything in season. This was a Monday in season and he agreed to do it—he was a good guy in that way. He wasn't happy about it; I remember him grumbling at me the whole way—with the cigar in his mouth—"I don't do anything in season."

He transcended football and was famous even in racing.

We sat down in a room full of about a thousand people, and he got up there and was the most sparkling, pleasant speaker. He just turned it on in front of all those people. He lived up to his commitment; he didn't really have to because he never did things in season. But he did it and he really wowed the whole crowd. He knew how important it was—all of our competitors, customers, and retailers were there. He was a very interesting guy.

The biggest coup of the whole campaign was when Kyle Petty was going to run in the Daytona 500 and Mike Ditka was brought down to be an honorary member of Petty's crew. He was wearing the Peak jacket, the uniform—all that stuff. He was so big at the time that CBS, who was broadcasting the race, made a big deal about Mike Ditka being at the Daytona 500; they even brought him up to the booth and interviewed him. He transcended football and was famous even in racing.

Announcer Tim Green, an eight-year NFL veteran, was a valedictorian at Syracuse and has written four football-related books. He is the only valedictorian in NFL history.

photo courtesy of Old World Industries

THE DOMINANT PLAYER
TOM HURVIS

Tom Hurvis is the founder and chairman of Old World Industries, which makes Peak Performance Antifreeze.

I had a very good relationship with Ditka and I like the guy a lot. You either like him or you don't like him. Ditka was on Kyle Petty's pit crew at Daytona and we got incredible press. He was on the ten o'clock news everywhere in the country, and it didn't cost us a penny except for what we paid Ditka. He loved it; NASCAR loved it. It was an incredible promotion.

When we were talking to Ditka about going down to Daytona, he said, "Earnhardt makes two and a half million dollars. I gotta meet that guy."

So we took him down to Daytona, and he was like a magnet there. It was right before the race and all the drivers came out of their pits and huddled around him. Then Earnhardt came up behind him and gave him a shot in the shoulder with his elbow. Ditka turned around, and they hugged each other. They had never met. It just shows you the tremendous respect people have for Ditka.

He had a lot of guts and did exactly what he wanted to do.

I was in the helicopter that brought Gretzky down from San Francisco to Ditka in LA, where Ditka gave this great speech about how he met Gretzky and how Gretzky slaughtered him up in Canada. Ditka was coaching junior hockey and Gretzky scored twenty goals in the first quarter.

Once, we were shooting a commercial in Chicago with Ditka, Gretzky, and Petty. Gretzky and Petty were there for about fifteen minutes, and everybody was looking at them and talking. Then Ditka came in and it was like Gretzky and Petty had disappeared. All of a sudden, he took over. He was the animal; he was the dominant player.

What was unusual about those guys was that every one of them was a terrific interview. Actually, the smoothest was Petty, but Gretzky was damn good. Ditka was so impatient about everything. You'd take one shot and that would be it; he'd say, "Well, hell, you took it once."

One day I got this phone call from Ditka, and he said, "Tom, this relationship's gotta change. I didn't get my check." I said, "Well, Mike, I sent the check to you." He was really pissed and he said, "You're probably going to ruin this whole relationship that we have." So I said, "Look, I sent it to you. I don't know what happened, but I sent it to you." I hung up the phone and called his secretary. She hadn't given it to him yet. So he would have just ripped my head off for nothing.

I was on the board of his charity. I never socialized with him but we had extremely good rapport. He said, "Look, Tom, I'll push Peak as much as I can, just send me a set of golf clubs and shirts." We had a very good relationship; I liked Ditka because I'm pretty direct, too. I loved the fact that the guy was pretty candid and said exactly what was on his mind. I know a lot of people really don't like Ditka. He was a wild man and he drank a lot—I know all about his failures—but the guy's honest. He's straightforward and says it like it is, and I like that. I love the guy; I think he had a lot of guts and did exactly what he wanted to do. He did a good job—he won the Super Bowl.

The revenue from one home football game at schools like Michigan and Tennessee pay for all the athletic scholarships in all their sports for the entire school year.

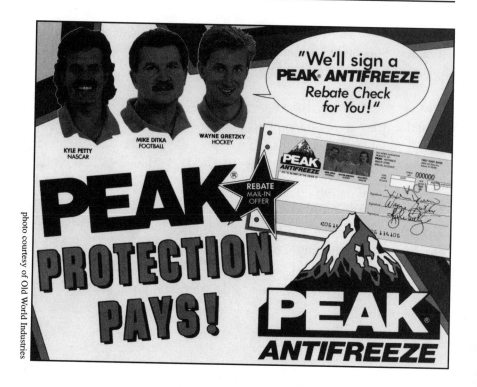

DITKA AND THE PRETTY BOY
MAC CHURCHILL

Mac Churchill, retired now in Naples, Florida, was the ad genius at J. Walter Thompson who decided to put Wayne Gretzky, Mike Ditka, and Kyle Petty together for Peak Performance Antifreeze in the mid-'80s.

Kyle had long hair; he was a hippie type at the time. Every woman alive walks into a room and falls in love with Kyle. He's a very handsome guy—he could have been a movie star.

Ditka walked in, and there's this guy who's almost pretty, and I thought, "Geez, this may not work well." But by the end of the first day of shooting, they became truly good friends. At first, I wasn't sure how it would work. I could imagine Ditka saying, "Aw, this is one of those pretty boys."

photo courtesy of Old World Industries

photo courtesy of Kyle Petty

DOING IT RIGHT THE FIRST TIME
KYLE PETTY

Kyle Petty has carved out his own superlative career on the NASCAR circuit, following in the footsteps of his father, Richard Petty.

Ditka ended up on my pit crew because we were both spokespersons for Peak Antifreeze, out of Des Plaines, Illinois. I drove a racecar for them and had for a couple of years. When Chicago went on their tear with the Bears, I became the East Coast and Southeast spokesperson for Peak. Ditka did the Midwest and Wayne Gretzky did California and Canada. Peak brought Ditka down one year for the race and he gave the team a pep talk. We were running like junk, we were terrible, but he gave us a pep talk before we ran the race and we thought we could beat the world. It was pretty cool to be around somebody who motivated like that.

We did a couple of commercials together, and I thought he was a great guy. When we were doing the commercials, he was very intense and focused on what he was doing. I get a little out in left field sometimes and just have a good time, so I'm not as intense as he is. We would go in and they would give us our lines. He's so intense that he wants to do it right the first time. He wants to please and he wants to do it right. But I could never tell if he was doing it right, or if the director was just afraid to tell him to do it again.

I saw him again after he had his heart attack, and he was a different person. He wasn't as intense; he was enjoying life and having a better time. The first time we worked together, he was a bit upset if we were supposed to start at 1:00 and we didn't start until 1:15. The second time, if we started at 1:15, he was okay.

He was in our pit at the Daytona race in '89 or '90, and he came down and saw

> **I could never tell if he was doing it right, or if the director was just afraid to tell him to do it again.**

the guys do a pit stop. It's pretty incredible to watch a group of guys go over a wall and change four tires and put twenty-one gallons of gas in a car in about sixteen or seventeen seconds. I think he had a new respect not only for what the racecar drivers did, but for what the pit guys did, too. Racing is a team sport, just like football was at the time.

All football fans have heard of Ditka, so I knew who he was. I'm a huge football fan, and I follow the conference that he coached in because I've always been a Packers fan.

I have not seen Ditka in person—only on TV in those dreadlocks— since those days. I have to admit: he looked good in the dreadlocks. And even if he didn't look good, you're not going to hear Kyle Petty say he didn't look good, because he's a pretty big guy.

Pete Rozelle never let an NFL game start later than 4:00 P.M. local time, other than the Monday night game, so that little kids could see the entire game before bedtime.

WILLING THE TEAM
DAVE McGINNIS

Mike Ditka was at his best when things were really tight. During a lot of ballgames in Chicago, he would basically will the team through the game. I can remember the first ballgame after the strike in 1987. The strike year was very, very hard in Chicago. We had started off the season 4–0. We were completely ahead of everyone. Then came the strike. The union held all their strike meetings in Chicago. When we came back, it was a very tense situation. Then we went down to play Tampa Bay. Of course, Tampa was having a hard time ever even scoring on the Bears, and we found ourselves down in the ballgame.

I can remember Mike standing up at halftime and saying, "Regardless of what has gone on in the past, you and we are still the Chicago Bears. You are the Chicago Bears, and you will be victorious." Once we went out there on the field, he went up and down the sideline, and it was like he was willing us. Neal Anderson would make a first down just by about the length of the football, and Ditka was right there on the sideline. If Neal Anderson needed four yards, Ditka was standing at four and a half to bring him across to that part. And we ended up winning that ballgame.

I can also remember a Monday night ballgame when we played Houston in the Astrodome. P. T. Willis got sacked right before halftime and Ditka was just livid. He came in the locker room, picked up a laundry cart full of towels—there's no telling how much it weighed—and just threw the laundry cart. The strength coach came over afterward and asked him, "Coach, can I get you something to drink?" He said, "Yeah, I need something to drink. I need some poison." Then the strength coach, who is very strong, tried to move the laundry cart back over to where it was supposed to be, and he couldn't pick it up.

When Vince Tobin got the defensive coordinator's job in 1986, Mike told Vince he wanted to hire a young linebacker coach. He brought several guys in to interview. Vince brought me in because I had been associated with Vince at Missouri.

I came in and started talking to him. Ditka said, "I have talked to some people about you." This was right after they had won the Super Bowl, and he said, "Now, tell me, if we're out there on the field, and you're coaching Mike Singletary, Otis Wilson, and Wilber Marshall—does that make any difference to you, or does making them better players than they are today make a difference to you?" I said, "Coach, I want to make them better players than they are today." He said, "Never, ever forget that. Never forget that. You're the guy I want for the job."

> Tex Schramm's first name is "Texas" even
> though he was born in California.

DITKA'S CITY LIGHTS
JIM RITTENBERG

Jim Rittenberg is one of the most successful restaurant and night-club owners in the history of the city of Chicago. He has started several dozen successful nightspots, including Juke Box Saturday Night and Faces, as well as starting Ditka's City Lights in the mid-'80s. Jim Rittenberg is the man who made Harry Caray the "Mayor of Rush Street." Jim now runs Mother Hubbard's restaurant in downtown Chicago.

I knew Ditka's City Lights was going to be busy; I had projections at five million. I had a great location—sixty thousand cars went by it every day. We opened in late '86 and I left in '91, and it closed about thirteen to fourteen months later. It wasn't going to be a celebrity joint until Jerry Vainisi approached us.

The nightclub was going to be called Faces, and the restaurant was going to be called Coach's Club. The restaurant was only 2,700 square feet of the 16,000 total square feet. Ditka's City Lights was a name I coined. I was trying to come up with a nightlife name for the nightclub. So we called it Ditka's Restaurant, and we called the back part City Lights Nightclub. That's where the big money was. I projected five million in the offering. I think we did $9.7 million one year.

I think Ditka added a good twenty-five to thirty percent to the gross, mostly for the restaurant business. The restaurant business is not as profitable as the nightclub business. Ditka was a pretty good sport about doing commercials for the restaurant. They were all pretty humorous. He did his Grabowski shuffle at the restaurant—that was kind of funny.

I would watch what he did, like the chewing gum incident in San Francisco. Then we went out and picked up all kinds of Wrigley chewing gum and handed it out to people after they ate dinner. When he had the heart attack, we came out with "Holy Mike's Mackerel." We tied in with the Heart Association and donated fifty cents from every order because mackerel is

When he had the heart attack, we came out with "Holy Mike's Mackerel."

very high in the acids that help prevent heart disease. When Buddy Ryan choked on a pork chop, I sent an order of pork chops to his hotel room when he was in town to play the Bears. I sent pork chops to Letterman to get him to talk about the restaurant on TV.

We were famous for our pork chops. The location I wanted was next to Carson's Rib Joint and surrounded by steak houses and pasta houses, so I needed a signature item that nobody else had. I couldn't do steaks because we had Morton's and Gene & Georgetti's. I couldn't do pasta because I was across from Leno's. I didn't want to do ribs because I was next door to Carson's Ribs. So I came up with pork chops. Everybody liked pork chops; it fit with the Ditka image. I said two is not enough, so I threw a third pork chop on the menu. They all yelled at me. They said, "Why are you putting a third pork chop on there?" I said, "Listen, this is what you're going to build a restaurant around." That was the beginning of the huge baked potatoes, too. It was more than anybody could eat: a baked potato the size of a football—a huge potato— and three pork chops rather than two, so you actually got a pound and a half of pork chops.

At Ditka's it was always jammed. We had a thing called The Coach's Club, and it was $40 for all you could eat and all you could drink when you watched the games on Sundays. I think that's what sparked those cornballs from "Saturday Night Live"—where they did "all you can eat when you watch the games." Those guys would sit around, dressed in Bears' colors. I've got to believe that somebody who came up with that idea had to have been in the restaurant.

Everybody liked pork chops; it fit with the Ditka image.

Every Sunday starting before kickoff at 11:30, we'd open the bar and a big buffet. The buffet had the pork chops and everything. It lasted until 3:30, until after the game was over. These guys had the same table every week and they dressed in the Bears' colors, and each week they'd get a prize—a hat or a T-shirt or something. They were diehards.

The NFL talked to me and said, "You can't show those games out of market; it's illegal." We were one of only two places in Chicago that had satellites. Gamekeepers on Armitage and Ditka's were the only two places. We had big screens and big satellite dishes. This was '85, '86, and '87; it hadn't been done yet.

The NFL said, "Not all our games are legal. We'd hate to have to bust a place with Ditka's name on it." I said, "Listen, if you make everybody else stop, I'll stop, but it isn't fair to stop me and not anybody else."

We just kept on showing them and the problem went away. They never enforced it. But later they came out with a plan where you had to pay for it. And that was fine with us.

They didn't have sports bloopers on tape then; we made our own sports bloopers. When people were waiting two hours for a table, we would run the sports bloopers to try to shorten their perception of time. We called the bloopers the "Ditka Dogs," since they all started with the dogs that run and jump over things and fall. We had a whole crew that did nothing but make bloopers. We had a TV and radio station—we did all our own editing and all our own production. The dancing waiters and waitresses in the nightclub were called "City Lights Skyliners." I actually had a choreographer work with them each week. So three or four times during the night we would stop, they would come out on the dance floor, and they would do a theme. Sometimes it would be a Chicago theme, sometimes an athletic theme, sometimes a Bears theme.

Ditka was nice to the people and came up to them. We used to have to cordon him off sometimes if there were too many people, but he was always nice to the little guys when they came up for autographs. He was always friendly. If he was impatient, he was impatient more or less with the staff. He wasn't like a Harry Caray, who would walk around from table to table, saying, "Hey, how are you?" "What's going on?" or "Hey, sweetheart. Give me a kiss." He wasn't a Harry Caray, but at the same time he was very positive, a real asset.

Ditka handled the football market. I hired Doug Buffone to represent us. That was interesting. When we did the parties, people would ask, "Will Coach Ditka be there?" If Coach Ditka wasn't going to be there, he'd make sure one of the players or one of his ex-teammates was there. It was always Doug Buffone. If Coach couldn't make it, he'd call his pal, Doug Buffone, and Doug would come down.

We had a tape made up of Doug Buffone, "Old No. 55," we called it, because a lot of people didn't know who Doug Buffone was. Doug was a great player, and we'd show him smashing heads, etc.

> Dean Cain, who played Superman on TV,
> holds the NCAA record for most
> interceptions in one season.

If Coach Ditka wasn't going to be there, he'd make sure one of the players or one of his ex-teammates was there.

We'd say, "And here he is, ladies and gentlemen, to say hello to you—Coach Ditka's best buddy, Doug Buffone." Doug would come in and say, "Coach called me yesterday to come down. He couldn't make it today, but you guys are important," and we'd pay Doug a fee. Doug was happy because at the time it was a nice little gig for him. He and I were friends for years.

We also had Leon Spinks working for us at Ditka's City Lights. Johnathan Brandemeir was a real hot disk jockey in town, and Johnathan needed someone to get Leon a job here in Chicago. He said, "If you can get him a job, I'll give you so much press and so much PR. It doesn't make any difference what you pay him, I'll give you ten times that."

So I had a meeting with Brandemeir and Leon Spinks, and we decided to hire Leon. We paid Leon—no secret—$700 a week. We put him in a tuxedo and we had a tape made up of when he beat Muhammad Ali for the championship. We'd show the last round, when he beat Ali. Then we'd say, "And now, ladies and gentlemen, I'd like you to welcome our host here at Ditka's Restaurant, Leon Spinks." Then Leon would come out. Now, people loved Leon, he was so friendly. Leon would walk around, shake hands, smile, pose for pictures. But Leon didn't do the parties. I still had Doug Buffone for the parties, and I had Leon going out and doing appearances for the restaurant.

That was his job, he was a PR figure. It really helped because we had a lot of Europeans come into the place from the hotels. They don't know what a Ditka was. When you think about it—he's a football coach. That's good. But he's one of twenty-eight football coaches, and Leon Spinks was one of four living heavyweight champions of the world, so we would introduce him. So these people from Europe would come from the hotels to see Leon Spinks.

Leon was just a hoot. A part of his deal was that he could eat for free. So I caught him walking out with lobsters and pork chops; he would go back in the kitchen and the guys were afraid to say no to him.

- George Halas and Marv Levy are the only men in their 70s to have coached NFL teams.
- Levy is the only head coach in any major sport to be Phi Beta Kappa.

photo courtesy of NBC/Paul Drinkwater

A STRAIGHTFOR-WARD GUY
BOB COSTAS

This Long Island native and St. Louis resident has handled a wide array of assignments since joining NBC in 1980. Just prior to that he called play-by-play for the Chicago Bulls' telecasts.

Ditka was seemingly straightforward. He was more likely than most people on television to say what he really felt about something. There was less of a filter between his first honest thought and what he might say, which is one of the reasons for his popularity. It may be the reason why he sometimes got himself into controversy. People found a genuineness in him, because he gave an honest reaction rather than a carefully thought-through presentation.

I have played golf with Ditka in the past. He was always amused by my ineptitude and how poorly I played. I'm a little better now. He was a great joker and storyteller; there was a different joke or story for each of the eighteen holes. He has difficulty with his knee or hip, and was limping around quite a bit. He's not as competitive on the golf course. He wanted to play well, but he was not competitive. He has always been great and friendly to me.

THE BIG LEBOWSKI
BUDDY DILIBERTO

photo courtesy of Buddy Diliberto/WWL 870AM

Buddy Diliberto has been a fixture in the New Orleans sports scene for many years and did radio shows with Mike Ditka before Ditka became head coach of the Saints.

On Wednesday nights during the football season, Ditka would fly down. He was actually working through Casino Magic then. They'd play golf with some of the high rollers, and I'd do that hour show on WWL with Mike from Casino Magic in Bay St. Louis, Mississippi, in '94 and '95, before he had anything to do with the Saints.

Actually, it was through that show in '95 that I realized how much he wanted to get back in the game. He was bitching about it and I said, "Are you really serious?" He said, "Yeah." So I went to see the governor. I had been so critical of the Saints operation I was sort of persona non grata, so I couldn't go to the Saints owner because he wouldn't give me the time of day. So I inquired who had the owner's ear. It was Governor Edwards, the guy who got DeBartolo kicked out of the league. I made a phone call and went up to visit with him for about an hour, telling him why I thought Ditka would be a good fit here.

He endorsed the idea and said he would talk to Benson about it. That was during the '95 season. At the end of the '95 season,

Benson didn't make a move. Everyone expected he was going to fire Jim Mora and make a move at that time. But he kept everybody for another year—well, it turned out not to be a full year because Mora quit in the middle of the '96 season. The governor told me he then talked to Benson.

I was convinced Ditka would be a good coach because of his background and because of all that he had accomplished in Chicago with the Super Bowl team. One thing I was convinced about—and this was proven right—I knew he'd be very marketable. I'm still keeping an open mind as to what kind of coach I think he is. I know this town because I'm a native and I knew that the sale of the Saints' season tickets was going into a freefall. I knew if you brought in Mike Ditka, all of a sudden this town would jump on the bandwagon again. Now, like everything else, within two or three years he's got to do something on the field, otherwise that confidence starts dwindling. So consequently, in my opinion, 1999 is sort of a watershed year. I don't think the owner will fire him, but as far as the confidence of the community is concerned, this is a watershed year.

I call him The Big Lebowski. You saw that movie; to me, that's exactly what he is. Here's an example: The week of the draft, they had this press conference and everyone was asking, "Would Mike do this, draft that guy?" They have it every year, so Ditka was sitting up there with the Director of Scouting. Anyway, I asked the question, and they went on about how they were doing everything they could to move up so they could get Ricky Williams. I asked the question, "Suppose that doesn't work; you can't make that deal,

> Q: What is in the NFL penalty flags that make them go straight down instead of fluttering?
> A: Uncooked popcorn. When an official throws his flag and then sees another infraction, he throws his cap.

nobody'll go for it, and you don't get a shot at Ricky Williams? Somebody else drafts him. But the other running back, Edgerrin James, if he is there when you all pick, would you go for him?" Ditka's answer was, "Well, he's a good back, but you know we've got Troy Davis. I don't see any difference in those two." Well, only a Big Lebowski would say something like that. I mean, you have Troy Davis come in and he absolutely embarrasses us and runs nowhere.

He chewed the guy out just like he would chew a quarterback out after he had thrown an interception.

He talked about how everybody was going to gang up on Ricky Williams. So consequently, he's trying to field the type of passing game they're going to have this year. He wants his quarterbacks to complete sixty-five percent of their passes. If anybody's watching the quarterbacks the Saints have, they couldn't complete sixty-five percent on the sidelines playing pitch and catch. The fact of the matter is, very few quarterbacks in the league, no matter who they are, ever complete sixty-five percent of their passes. I don't think he ever thinks before he talks.

It was great when we had our radio show. He wasn't in coaching then, so he would give very candid and humorous opinions. Now, with the shoe on the other foot, he was telling me recently how negative I am. I'm negative. And I burst out laughing. He didn't think I was negative in '94 and '95.

We were doing a show on WWL, the biggest station in the area, so the casino wanted to get a sports show on WWL. They went with the idea that they could deliver Mike Ditka if WWL would put it on. WWL's point at the time was "Why do we want Mike

I don't think he ever thinks before he talks.

Ditka? We've got Buddy, he's our sports talk guy. Everything's going fine as far as ratings and everything like that." From that, they said, "Why don't we put the two of them together?" So consequently, Casino Magic was the one who delivered Ditka. Naturally, my attitude was "Absolutely, I'd love to do that." I had never really met him—I had done interviews with him, like in the Super Bowl when they were playing New Orleans. I grew up with Richie Petitbon; we're real good friends. We vacation together almost every year. He had played with him and I knew a lot about him. But other than doing interviews with him, I had never really met him until those shows in the casino.

Usually after the show we would go over to the dice table and play some dice. He's a big player on the dice table. One particular night the dice table was pretty filled, but Ditka got his bets all over the place. One person got the dice, and he was obviously not interested in the game—he was talking to the girl next to him. Well, it was his turn to roll the dice and he just kind of flings them out— sort of a limp fling—and he's not paying attention to the game. All of a sudden, Ditka yells at him from the other end of the table, "Goddamn it, if you want to play dice, roll the dice like you mean something, like you want to play, instead of that little flicking kind of thing." The guy's mouth opened like the end of the Mississippi. He chewed the guy out just like he would chew a quarterback out after he had thrown an interception—after he had done something the coach had told him not to do. The freaking guy almost died just listening to the cussing. The rest of us at the table just kind of smiled.

After one of the games last year, Ditka was so upset at the blocking of his wide receivers that on Monday when he had his press conference, he said that the Country Day wide receivers blocked better than our wide receivers. Country Day is a little private school that's about a mile away from the Saints camp. I do a show with him every Tuesday night at the restaurant, and who shows up but the whole corps of Country Day wide receivers to offer him their services. Man, he got a big kick out of that. We put them on live: "We heard you needed us, and we want to help. We're ready to suit up."

Red Grange was not the most famous person coached by the legendary Bob Zuppke. When Zuppke coached high school football in suburban Chicago, one of his players was Ernest Hemingway.

photo courtesy of SCORE radio 1160AM

AN AVERAGE GUY
MIKE NORTH

Mike North has been a fixture on Score radio and in sports talk radio in Chicago for the last ten years.

About three years ago, I was hosting a golf tournament for the Italian-American Sports Hall of Fame on the South Side of Chicago. Ditka called me the night before the tournament and asked me if I wanted to go to Bay St. Louis, Mississippi. I was hosting the golf outing on a Wednesday; on Tuesday night he called and said, "Hey, kid, how'd you like to go to Bay St. Louis, Mississippi, with me tomorrow? I got a radio show to shoot with Buddy Diliberto. It's from Casino Magic."

Well, I'm just a regular guy—I'm not used to this. I asked, "What are we going to do, take United?" He said, "No, no, no. Meet me at Palwaukee airport." So I left the golf outing at about 2:00 to be at Palwaukee airport at 3:30. We jumped on this Lear jet and flew to Mississippi. There was a buffet on the plane, and his wife, my wife, and another couple were with us. We flew out there and took a limo from the airport in Mississippi.

He didn't have to do the show until 6:30, so we did a little gambling. Then we did this hour-long radio show—me, him, and Diliberto. Afterward, we ate, and I was back home in Chicago by 10:30 and watching the Letterman show. That's the way the guy is. He just jumps on flights, spends maybe four hours somewhere, and then leaves. I'm not used to this kind of thing—I can't believe it.

If you look at the Bear logo and a picture of him, there's not much difference. He's a human being in a bear's hat.

I golfed with him in the Score golf outing, and one of my shots almost hit him on the head. He was on the foursome in front of me. He turned around, and I almost had a heart attack. He said, "Who did that?" Nobody would answer.

The first year I worked for him, each host for the Score did a week with him from his restaurant in Chicago. I did the show with him and we got into this philosophical football argument. He said to me during a commercial break, "How come you're not afraid of me?" I had never met the guy, but I always respected him and loved him as a coach. I said, "Because my dad was tougher than you. Why would I be afraid of you when I wasn't afraid of my dad?" Ever since then we got along great. He intimidated a lot of the hosts. He scares players when they walk in to see him in his office. Most guys are intimidated by him. But I think that's what makes it fun. He's a big guy, and he looks like a bear—he looks like the Bears logo. If you look at the Bear logo and a picture of him, there's not much difference. He's a human being in a bear's hat.

I loved him when I was growing up in Chicago; he left in 1966. We loved him as kids. We saw him catch touchdown passes in Dallas. But when he got the job with the Bears, we were all thrilled. All the writers in Chicago thought he'd only last a year, because of his feistiness, because they didn't think he could do it, because he was a special teams coach. They thought Halas picked the wrong guy— they didn't think he had the mental makeup to be a coach. But he was exactly the guy the Bears needed. He still is the biggest name in Chicago next to Michael Jordan.

He's an average guy. He'll still go out, hang around, have drinks. He's been in Chicago for the last month. He's the New Orleans coach, but he's in Chicago all the time. He's got a restaurant here; you see him on Rush Street. He's a big kid, that's what he is. He's a cool guy to hang out with. He comes across as a blue-collar guy, even though he's got all the money in the world. He reminds me of a guy who would live in a bungalow on the southwest side. He's that kind of guy.

He's a great speaker when he does commercials. He never makes a mistake; he does everything in one take whether it's radio or TV. He's very intelligent.

He and Harry were at Ditka's O'Hare, doing a Budweiser spot, and Ditka did his line perfectly. Now, Ditka's one of those guys who, once he does it, he wants to go. But he had to stay in the commer-

> The Rams, who began as the Cleveland Rams, were named for the Fordham University team.

cial spot because Harry kept flubbing his lines. Harry'd say, "I'm sorry, Mike." And Ditka would say, "Come on, Harry, take your time, you'll get it done." Twenty minutes later, Harry was still screwing up his lines. But they finally got it done. You could see that Mike was becoming impatient even though he loved Harry, because Mike Ditka doesn't waste any time. He wanted in and he wanted out. It was hilarious to listen to those two do the outtakes.

> # He should have never been let go as Bears coach.

He should have never been let go as Bears coach. I think we would be a playoff team right now if he hadn't been let go. Every coach who has been at a place for any amount of time has had bad times— like Shula. Things happen, it's cyclical, but Ditka would have had them back on their feet already. Since he's been gone, nothing's gone right.

There are still guys who, like him, have the killer instinct. The Bill Parcells, the Bobby Knights, and people like that prove that the days of the Ditkas aren't gone. But I think there are less than more. If Ditka was still head coach of this team, there'd still be rabid interest in him. None of the common guys wanted him fired. The common people, the blue-collar guys, never wanted him fired. He had two losing seasons, and McCaskey couldn't wait for him to lose; McCaskey was afraid of him. So McCaskey got rid of him instead of trying to work things out. I think the only fault Ditka had was that he thought he was never going to get fired. That's why he never tried to play politics, though he's not that kind of guy anyway. He's not going to BS anybody. He's a straight-shooting guy, and that's what I love about him.

photo courtesy of *Chicago Tribune*

LEARNING UNDER GOD'S COACH

SKIP BAYLESS

Skip is an Oklahoma City native, a Vanderbilt graduate, a long-time Dallas sports writer, and now a columnist for the Chicago Tribune. *He is the author of several best-selling sports books, including* God's Coach *and* The Boys.

A friend of mine and I went out to play golf in Dallas in March 1981, in early spring. We got to the club and some big cold front blew through, what we used to call a norther in Dallas. The temperature dropped, the wind kicked up, and the wind chill was probably in the 20s or 30s. We were having lunch, watching this happen, and we said, "That's enough, we're not going to play today." It would have been our first time to play that spring. We continued having lunch, talking and laughing about how people were driving off the course in their carts because they just couldn't take it anymore.

As we sat there, we could see up the ninth fairway. There was one guy left, playing his way toward the clubhouse up number nine. We both remarked that the guy must be an idiot to still be out there playing by himself. The wind was blowing into his face. He was just hitting shot after shot up the fairway into the teeth of the wind. It was blowing so hard he was having trouble advancing the ball. Anyone would in that kind of wind—it was forty miles per hour.

The guy finally got up on the green, which was near the window where we were sitting, and I looked down and said, "I think that's Mike Ditka," who at that point was not a big deal in Dallas because he was a special teams coach. I was amazed that it was Mike Ditka who was still out there playing in that wind.

Not only did he putt out, but he got in his cart, drove past our window, and went to the tenth tee. He was still going, and he kept playing through the afternoon in that wind chill. Maybe people in Chicago would have thought it was like springtime, but to us in Dallas, it was too cold to be playing golf. Probably too cold to be playing football.

When Mike Ditka was Landry's receivers' coach, a story circulated in the locker room about what a "crazy mother" Ditka was. After one practice, as the receivers ran halfhearted sprints, Ditka challenged them to a fistfight. Right there, all at once—Drew Pearson, Butch Johnson, Tony Hill, Billy Joe DuPree, Doug Cosbie. "Come on, you pussies!" Ditka yelled as Landry looked on. There were no takers.

Now, of course, it seems that every other Saints practice ends with Coach Ditka challenging half the squad to a rumble. But in the Cowboys structure, Ditka seemed to have enough loose screws to build an entire robot. He was Landry's token maniac.

But Ditka also was as shrewd as Tex Schramm. He knew he could get away with an occasional explosion as long as he paid the proper homage to Mount Landry. Ditka kissed Landry's, well, hat. All Landry's top assistants did—Ditka, Dan Reeves, John Mackovic,

Academic All-American teams have been picked every year since 1952. Nebraska leads all colleges by a wide margin in number of players selected.

Gene Stallings. Today they tell interviewers that coaching under Landry was among their "greatest" experiences, but it wasn't then. One thing they learned in Dallas was that it isn't always wise to be honest, especially about legends.

Ditka seemed to have enough loose screws to build an entire robot. He was Landry's token maniac.

When they were under Landry, they always filled newspaper stories with awe over him. They publicly accepted their ridiculously limited amount of input and responsibility. They arrived early for coaches' meetings and mostly deferred to Landry's one-way thinking. "Assistants," Drew Pearson said, "could act like little kids, peeking around the corner to see if Landry was coming. They were even more afraid of him than the players were. Once when I was coaching, my daughter didn't have a ride home from school, and I absolutely had to go get her and miss some of practice. The other assistants said, 'You can't miss practice.' They thought I was crazy. But I just said, well, I'll have to suffer the consequences. Coach Landry didn't really say anything."

But Pearson, who lasted just one year as an assistant, had no life-or-death ambition to become a head coach. The others knew that if they could live with their head coach, they'd have a better chance of becoming one. Serving under God's Coach made for a blinding resume. If an assistant was good enough for Tom Landry, he was good enough for an owner in search of a Landry.

One morning at camp I wandered into the TV room of the coaches' dorm and found Ditka intently watching a soap opera.

"You always watch this?" I asked.

"Don't tell anybody," Ditka said, grinning. He eyed me a second and said, "You don't swallow the party line around here, do you? I like that." And Ditka winked at me.

Associating with God's Coach certainly didn't hurt "crazy" Ditka. When the Bears called Ditka in 1982, several Chicago writers called me to ask if the guy was sane. I told them I wasn't sure he had enough of a handle on his temper to last as a head coach, but I stressed that Ditka knew how to play the game, both on the field and behind the microphone.

As Bears coach, Ditka actually became a phone pal of Landry's. They talked once or so a week. Landry volunteered to serve as a character witness when Ditka was arrested for DWI in 1985. You got the feeling Landry wished he could be a little more like Ditka, not to intoxication, but a little more spontaneous and outwardly emotional. But did Ditka and Reeves keep in touch with Landry the way you do with a tough professor or a commanding officer? It's difficult to imagine Ditka or Reeves calling Landry to shoot the breeze or, for that matter, Landry chatting at length with anyone but Alicia. But in a profession without much security or mercy, continuing a relationship with Landry can't hurt your image.

Landry delighted in talking to the media about the success of his "sons," Ditka and Reeves, especially as the Cowboys were less and less successful. But he never was able to replace what Ditka and Reeves did for his Cowboys teams. They could keep a Butch Johnson from flying off the handle and the lid from flying off Landry's locker room.

> Rich Kotite, former head coach of the Eagles
> and the Jets, was once Muhammad Ali's
> sparring partner in Miami.

Doug Todd and Greg Aiello   photo courtesy of *Dallas Cowboys Weekly*

AMERICA'S TEAM

GREG AIELLO

Greg Aiello is a fine Notre Dame man who used to be the Public Relations Director for the Dallas Cowboys. Now he's the head of Public Relations for the National Football League.

The term "America's Team" for the Dallas Cowboys came into play when Ditka was coaching in Dallas. My colleague, Doug Todd, who died a couple of years ago, actually came up with the phrase and put it on a NFL Films highlight show. It was 1979, the year I got there. Doug came up with the term, but we always just passed it off on NFL Films so it wouldn't sound too arrogant.

The Cowboys had been to five Super Bowls; in their fifth Super Bowl of the '70s, they lost in a 35–31 game to Pittsburgh. It was January, in the 1978–79 season, and they were trying to come up with some concept for the film because they had lost the Super Bowl. They had won it the year before. Bob Ryan actually came up with the theme—that the Cowboys had transcended Dallas and were a national team. They had all this footage of the Cowboys and their fans on the road, and they were batting around ideas for what to call the team. Doug Todd came up with "America's Team." They decided that was the one.

> **Mike Ditka was sort of the anti-Landry in a lot of ways.**

It was during that 1979 season that it started to catch on. When we went on the road, writers just started picking up on the idea, and we helped sell it. The Cowboys were the most popular team at that time. We promoted it and the media responded to it because it was legitimate. It was a phenomenon.

What I remember about Mike Ditka in those Dallas days were the characteristics that everyone later came to enjoy and appreciate after he went to Chicago and became a national celebrity. I remember his intensity, his emotions, and the way he could express himself.

He and Dan Reeves were big buddies. They were partners; they'd played together. And now they were young coaches under Tom Landry, so they ran around together. Ditka was considered sort of half-crazy. If you were with the Cowboys, a head coach was supposed to be like Tom Landry, and Mike Ditka was sort of the anti-Landry in a lot of ways. He was so emotional and intense and seemingly out of control at times, to the point where no one in Dallas really envisioned Mike Ditka as a future head coach, because Tom Landry was the model.

And yet the interesting thing was that Tom loved Ditka. Maybe because Tom appreciated that Ditka had things that Tom didn't have, in terms of his way of expressing himself and his intensity—his emotions. Tom also appreciated his commitment to the game and his passion for football.

They seem like opposites, but yet Tom really loved Ditka. So it was somewhat surprising when all of a sudden he was named the head coach of the Bears. And he was a special teams coach with Dallas. That's somewhat of an unusual jump, going from special teams coach to head coach. It was somewhat surprising in that sense, but he went on to enjoy great success and is an outstanding football leader.

In my first year with Dallas, we played up at Pittsburgh. This was a big rivalry at the time; they were the defending Super Bowl champs. We played two Super Bowls against them. There was a little scuffle along our sideline involving Ron Johnson—I think he was a rookie cornerback with the Steelers—and Dikta came running up the sideline with a football in his hand and sort of leaned over and fired this football at Ron Johnson's head. The official threw a flag for a fifteen-yard penalty. That's something Tom Landry would never do. And something you wouldn't expect a head coach to do. But it was part of Dikta's intensity.

Bronko Nagurski played nine years for the Chicago Bears and had exactly one one hundred-yard rushing game.

A FRIEND FOR LIFE
DAVE McGINNIS

photo courtesy of *Dallas Cowboys Weekly*

Mike Ditka and his wife were extremely good to my wife and I the whole time we were in Chicago. Mike Ditka has done so much for me during my career—even today I could pick up the phone and call him and ask for anything, and he would do it.

When he got out, you knew—because of the way the situation was when it ended and because of his resolve and how strong a personality he is—you knew that he would be back in the ballgame.

People don't even know the extent of what Mike Ditka has done in his charitable works. To see him around those kids in Misericordia, how involved he was and how gentle he was—it's incredible. The strength coach on the Bears' staff during the time Ditka was there had a child who was born diagnosed with Down's syndrome. I remember Mike Ditka going to that coach's house, talking to them and sitting and holding that child. Just to see Mike holding that little girl and being as loving as he was—these are things that people don't know, that he's really a wonderful, wonderful man who is very well grounded.

I can remember when we were coaching at the Senior Bowl one year, and he would take us out, as a staff, every night to eat. It was out of the question for anybody but Mike to pay. And the way he is treated—it was like moving around the city of Mobile every night with a rock star, because of the way the people reacted when they saw him.

When Ditka enters a place, everybody recognizes and knows and identifies with him immediately.

We went overseas to play; we went to Berlin, to Sweden, to London. When Ditka enters a place, everybody recognizes and knows and identifies with him immediately. I can remember one time in Goteberg, Sweden, when we all came back from dinner and sat down in the lobby of a Swedish hotel. Before we knew it, it was midnight and there had to be four hundred people in that lobby, just sitting, and Mike was not holding court, but involving everybody in what was going on. He has that type of personality that draws everything to him. It was like being with a rock star.

I can remember the first year Mike put on a golf tournament in Aliquippa, and we all went back there. Some of the best times we had were at the Old Mill Inn. There were guys sitting there who knew Ditka when he was little and were talking to him about the time he chased his brother around the Little League field. And Mike would sit right there with them.

That is the plus of the man: he has gotten so large, yet he has retained who he really is and that is what endears him to so many people. That's why I count him as a very good friend and why we are so close, because he has got deep, deep roots and deep values, he is a spiritual guy, and he is so loyal. If you are loyal to Mike Ditka, you have got a friend for life. He is so solid and so grounded, and he has got so much—as we say in west Texas—bottom to him and so much inside of him. Immediately, if you are that kind of person, people are going to attach themselves to you. To this day, I know I can believe what Mike Ditka tells me, and that he would do anything for me. All this about his temper, it's only because he wants everybody involved with him to be as passionate about what they're doing as he is.

I can remember when my wife and I got married in Chicago. I'm from west Texas; my wife is from Colby, in western Kansas. I invited Mike and Diana to the wedding and to the reception, just because it's what you do.

We got married on May 6, and it snowed that day, believe it or not. I remember Mike rented a limo and brought several office employees down to the wedding, stayed at the wedding, and then came to the reception. And it

If you are loyal to Mike Ditka, you have got a friend for life.

was not just a cursory appearance; he sat at that reception for three hours. He signed autographs for every little aunt from west Texas and western Kansas, took every picture—everything they wanted.

We had a nice reception at a hotel on the North Shore. A waiter said to me, "David, coach Ditka would like to buy some champagne for the reception." I said, "No, no, we've already got champagne for the reception." He said, "NO, COACH DITKA WANTS . . ." Obviously, he bought the best—Dom Perignon—and sat there, and it was the most gracious thing I have ever seen.

There was no telling how much money he was making for appearances at that time in his career. Yet he stayed there all day and signed autographs, posed for pictures, kissed little aunts and grandmas, and shook everybody's hand, and really just sat and mixed. It was a wonderful, wonderful thing. And I told him days afterward, "Mike, I sincerely appreciate it." He said, "David, I wouldn't have expected to do anything else. What did you expect?"

Mike is a guy who is very perceptive, and that's what makes you feel good. Once Mike Ditka counts you as a friend, he's very perceptive and he understands. It's just like you or I.

You can tell when someone is genuine or not. And that, I think, is his greatest attribute. He really is able to see. He knows which button to push on which players because he understands personalities. He knows. He's wonderful to watch, and I learned a lot as a young coach about the way he would push the buttons of individual players and then how he would push the button of the team as a whole— different ways, different times. He's a master at it, and you can see why he's a tremendous competitor, why he was so successful as a player, and now why he is so successful as a coach.

> The Rose Bowl parade originally had nothing to
> do with the Rose Bowl football game.
> It was a celebration in Pasadena for
> the ripening of the oranges.

DOING THINGS THE RIGHT WAY

VINCE TOBIN

photo courtesy of the Chicago Bears

Vince Tobin has been the head football coach of the Arizona Cardinals since the ouster of Buddy Ryan. Ironically, it was Tobin who had the unenviable task of replacing Buddy Ryan after the Bears' Super Bowl championship in 1986.

I grew up on a farm near Burlington Junction, Missouri, and played football at the University of Missouri. I worked for the Columbia Neighborhood Youth Corps in Columbia, which was part of the poverty program for the Great Society under Lyndon Johnson. The more money they poured into it, the more I became the guy who filled out paperwork and sent it to Washington. I didn't want to do it anymore, so I went and talked to the coaches to see if they could get me a high school coaching job. They were expanding their staff and they hired me as an assistant coach. I went right in and coached there for nine years. I left in 1977 and went to Canada to coach the BC Lions of the Canadian Football League for three years. When I left, I went to the USFL and worked with Jim Mora and the Philadelphia Stars for three years. We were 15–3 our first year and 16–2 our next year, and we won the championship two out of three years. We played in the championship game all three years. When that league folded, I went to Chicago and stayed there.

He tries to do things the right way and expects other people to do things the right way.

Before Buddy Ryan took the Philadelphia Eagles job in 1986, Jim Mora had an opportunity to take three jobs: he could have taken the Eagles job, the St. Louis job, or the New Orleans job. Jim Finks went to New Orleans. He had been the Bears' general manager and had hired my brother Bill, who worked for the Bears as their personnel director. When Finks went to New Orleans, he in turn called Jim Mora about taking the New Orleans job. Jim went down and accepted it. When Jim dropped out of the Philadelphia Eagles job, Buddy Ryan got it. I was on my way to New Orleans to be with Jim Mora. I hadn't signed a contract or accepted the job or anything.

Mike Ditka called me the night before I left to go to New Orleans and asked me if I'd be interested in coming to the Bears as an offensive coordinator. So I went down to New Orleans, met with Jim, and told him that Mike had called and I was interested in talking to him about a job. Ditka was coming down there for the scouting combine, so I met with him about two days after I had gotten to New Orleans and interviewed with him. He offered me the job and I accepted. It was a bang-bang thing—it's not like he interviewed a lot of people. He interviewed me and offered me the job.

With all that had happened, Mike never once second guessed me on any call. When I first started he said, "The defense is yours to do with as you see fit." I certainly respected him for that, because if I hadn't have had his support, it would have been a hard act to follow. We had some problems, but in '86 the team ended up better in almost every defensive statistic than they had in '85. We set the record in 1986 for the fewest points allowed, and that record still stands today.

Mike is a Christian. He believes very strongly that God has a plan for everybody's life and that He's got a plan for his life. Mike is very committed to that. As Mike will tell you, he tries to control his temper, but it sometimes gets the best of him. He tries to do things the right way and expects other people to do things the right way.

When the ax came down in Chicago in January 1993, we were all shocked. It was done very, very clumsily, after the season was over. The owner was gone and we were sitting there twisting in the wind for about eight or ten days until he came back. They released Mike, and it was a very emotional time.

We had had a down year that year, and it gave ownership an opening and they took advantage of it. Every team has down years, but they've had a down cycle ever since Ditka left, I know that.

> Barry Sanders was tackled for losses fourteen percent of the time. On approximately four hundred carries, he lost more than one thousand yards.

photo courtesy of *Dallas Cowboys Weekly*

DITKA ON FAME AND RELIGION

I do influence a lot of people, sometimes in a good way and sometimes in a bad way. I think the only way you can influence people is through your life, not by something they read about you. Some people are going to like it and some aren't. I get it all the time; I get people who are great fans, and I get people who don't like me at all. And that's fine. There's nobody who is totally liked, no matter who it is. There's somebody that will find something wrong with Ernie Banks—let's face it. People are like that.

My involvement with Misericordia started when someone invited me to a golf tournament and I met Sister Rosemary. She said, "Why don't you come visit the place?" I did, and I realized it's not so much what you give, but what you get. You get a lot more than you give. It's become the love of my life. I deal with an institution down here (in New Orleans) called St. Michael's School for Special Children. There's Sister Rosemary in Chicago, and there's Sister Lillian here. These are people who devote their lives to taking care of special children. Whether it be the Special Olympics or something else, people like that love unconditionally. As healthy human beings, we have a tendency to put special conditions on anything—especially our love: how much we're going to give, who we're going to give it to, why we're going to give it to them. We find problems with everything. We think, "Oh, he's good for this reason," or "He's bad for that reason." But the love of these children is unconditional. The Bible says: "Unless you become as little children you can't enter the kingdom of heaven." What the Bible is talking about is: simply the ability to love and to treat people with love. Kids don't find too many problems with anybody else—that's a fact. That's what He was saying.

I've got a long way to go in life. I've got a lot of problems. I work on them. I don't think people really care—and I'm being honest with you—what my religious preferences are. I am what I am. I've learned one thing: I can't worry too much about what people think about me in life. I really can't. I have enough trouble worrying about what I'm doing myself. What they think is not going to bother me a whole lot.

I don't believe the good things that are said about me and I don't believe the bad things that are said about me. What I do know is who I am and what I'm trying to do in life. Everybody knows everything there is to know about me. When the last chapter is written, it's going to be written in New Orleans.

Chapter 4

Tom Landry

Jim Stamborski

Grant DePorter

Butch McGuire

Dan Reeves

Chet Coppock

Don Pierson

Keith Buchert

Tom Dreesen

Robert Smigel

photo courtesy of *Dallas Cowboys Weekly*

Fans and Friends

A COMPETITIVE NATURE
TOM LANDRY

photo courtesy of Dallas Cowboys Weekly

The Dallas Cowboys were not the first NFL team to play in Texas. Before the Cowboys started in 1960, there was an NFL team that played in Dallas for one year in 1952. The franchise, formerly the New York Yanks franchise, moved to Dallas and became the Dallas Texans. In their very first game, their first touchdown was the result of a fumbled punt by a New York Giants player, Tom Landry, the same Tom Landry who would coach the Cowboys for the first twenty-nine years of their existence.

We got Ditka in '69 in an offseason trade with Philadelphia. He had been sent from the Bears to the Eagles a few years after he angered George Halas by considering a jump to the rival AFL. To be perfectly honest, when Mike came to the Cowboys, he wasn't worth shooting. His knees were bad, his legs were gone. But he worked diligently with our weight coach to build his legs back up to the point where he made a valuable contribution to the Cowboys' offense for the next several years. Mike immediately proved he was not only a smart player, but also a tough competitor who wouldn't let anything keep him from playing.

A little more than a week before the season opener, an automobile accident left Ditka shaken and badly bruised, and four of his front teeth loose. A dentist told Mike he should sit out for a few weeks to allow the teeth time to tighten back up.

Mike just looked at the man and said, "Pull them." The dentist decided to fit him with a special rubber mouthpiece instead. Mike played his first game as a Cowboy the next week.

To be perfectly honest, when Mike came to the Cowboys, he wasn't worth shooting.

After I was fired in 1989, my wife and I were at our home in Palm Springs, at the time when the NFL held its annual spring meetings in Palm Springs. We didn't go to any of the meetings, of course, but Mike and Diana Ditka, Dan and Pam Reeves, and Gene and Ruth Ann Stallings called and invited Alicia and I to join them for dinner at a local restaurant.

It felt like old times. Gene Stallings, an old Bear Bryant protégé out of the University of Alabama, worked with me for fourteen years before he left to become head coach of the Cardinals in 1986. He is a fine football man and a dear friend, and there's no one I respect more as a family man and a father than Gene.

Mike played and coached under me for thirteen years before he took over as coach of the Chicago Bears. Danny played and coached with me for sixteen years. The two of them were as much like sons as assistants. In fact, I sometimes had to give them a little stern fatherly advice.

I remember one day when they got so worked up at the officials that I sat them down after the game and said, "I think I'd rather lose a football game than ever have my assistants act that way on the sidelines again."

I don't know of anyone more fiercely competitive than Mike and Dan. And not just about football. I used to play a little tennis with them during training camps. For them, tennis was a contact sport. They'd rather knock their partner down trying to get to a drop shot than lose an uncontested point.

Even across the net from Mike you weren't safe. You never knew what he'd do if he missed a particularly frustrating shot. I've seen him smash his racket on the court until it looked like an aluminum pretzel, then bend it back into its approximate original shape and go on with the match. One day he blew a shot and angrily slung his racket at the net and missed, hitting me on the ankle and sending me hopping around the court on one foot.

They were just as competitive in whatever they did. Danny brought a dartboard to Thousand Oaks one year and hung it on the wall of his dorm room. He and Mike went at it with such a vengeance they had to pay for a new wall when we broke training camp.

So we had a lot of memories to talk about and a lot of laughter to share in that Palm Springs restaurant. In fact, our evening together was such a poignant reminder of all that we'd enjoyed, all the associations that would never be again, that Alicia broke down and cried for the first time since my firing. For my sake, she'd been so strong for so long. It was like everything finally hit her. A wonderful part of our life was really over. Sensing that completely, she finally let down and cried. But it was okay; we were among loving friends.

Q: What two college football teams play at Rice Stadium?
A: Rice University in Houston and the University of Utah in Salt Lake. Both stadiums are named Rice.

ONE OF US
JIM STAMBORSKI

Jim Stamborski defied all the odds and lived the dream of many sports fans. He wrote a book about his biggest sports hero—Mike Ditka.

I grew up in southern California. My father was transferred to Chicago in 1960, and that's when I became a Bears fan. The '60s were a time of great Bears teams, culminating in 1963 with the Bears' 14–10 championship victory over the Giants at Wrigley Field. From that point on, the Bears were my favorite team. I really liked Ditka and Bill Wade a lot. The Bears were a great team at that time—when they truly were "Monsters of the Midway."

It was fun following Ditka's career. Anyone who saw him play that season saw a very crucial game. Every time you see a Ditka highlight film, you see him plowing through the whole Steelers team and scoring a touchdown. That was a tremendous run; it was unbelievable.

You ask people in Aliquippa, Pennsylvania, about Mike, or people he has visited in the hospital when they were sick, or his friends and acquaintances, and they all have something really nice to say about him. This thing about his ex-players not liking him is a big fallacy, a big myth. Jim Harbaugh has nothing but the highest praise for Mike Ditka, and it's the same with Jim McMahon and Mike

Tomczak. You saw him grabbing their helmets or reaming them out on the sidelines, but they have a tremendous amount of respect for Mike, as do almost all the players who have played for him. It really is surprising when you consider his reputation of being a hard-nosed guy.

A lot of people forget that Mike Ditka played the game. He played the game as a Hall of Famer, and now he's a coach, so he knows what the game is about. He constantly talks to players about the love of the game, and tells them not to be in it just for the money. He was very upset when the players went on strike in '87, and he basically said that free agency was going to kill football. And if you look at it right now, free agency is a big problem. Ditka was right.

He is so popular because he is one of us— honest, hardworking.

He was right about Doug Flutie, too, and a lot of people don't give him credit for that. Everybody laughed when Mike drafted Doug Flutie, and look what he did. He went to the Canadian Football League, set all the records, came back to the NFL, and had an outstanding season for Buffalo. Nobody remembers that about Mike Ditka. Ditka tried to sign Flutie and Cunningham for New Orleans, too. Everybody laughed and said, "There's no way." But Ditka is a tremendous evaluator of talent, and he's a gambler, too. Look at this riverboat gamble with Ricky Williams. You've got to love it.

I think he is so popular because he is one of us—honest, hardworking, a guy who busted his ass to get where he wanted to go and is honest, straightforward, loyal, and a straight-shooter. He's had his ups and downs, just like all of us. He can walk into any bar, in any steel mill town, in Chicago, in New Orleans, or any other place, and sit down, have a shot and a beer with somebody, and talk about life.

He was a bust-out player, by his own admission, when he left the Bears. But he worked hard; he's a hard worker. He knows what it's like to have a boss who gives him a hard time. He knows what it's like to be a player. He knows what it's like to be a human being—to be out there, busting your ass to make a few dollars. That's what I like about Mike Ditka. He doesn't forget his roots. He's a steel mill kid. He'll tell you that he got to where he is by working harder than everybody else. That's what we're all about. That's what we have to do in life.

But he's done it with class, dignity, and honesty, and he's done it with great humor. Mike Ditka is atypical of a celebrity, and of course when you're different, people seem to gravitate to you because you're unusual. Any coach has his guarded moments—he will or won't say certain things. Ditka is unusual because he's an honest, straightforward, no-nonsense kind of guy. You never know what he is going to say, because he is totally and completely honest with his feelings. He will say things that, before they even come out of his mouth, he knows will upset people and get him in trouble.

But he'd say, "Hey, that's the way I am. Take it or leave it." When Ditka complained in the paper about Refrigerator Perry's wife cooking too much for him, he got reamed. But he came out and said, "I apologize. I've learned my lesson. I probably shouldn't have said it." That's the way he is; he just laid it all out there.

How many people do you know who are totally honest in the public eye and in private, too? That really intrigued me about Ditka. He doesn't care what he says as long as he feels it's honest. He doesn't care if it's not the politically correct thing to say. When he said recently that downtown New Orleans was full of trash and they should clean it up,

> Quarterback Chris Chandler is married to
> John Brodie's daughter.

it was true, but he got roasted for it. He got roasted for his honesty. That's what we admire—hard work, honesty, and loyalty. That's Mike Ditka.

Just before the playoff game with the Rams, somebody said, "How would you describe this game?" Ditka said, "Well, this is the Smiths versus the Grabowskis." Everybody laughed, and

> **"The Grabowskis know who they are. My team is full of Grabowskis."**

the guy said, "What do you mean by 'the Grabowskis'?" And Ditka said, "The Grabowskis know who they are. My team is full of Grabowskis." So of course, sociologists came on the scene and examined it, and one guy was pretty close when he said, "A Grabowski is a person who understands the sustained pushing of the rock up the hill." I thought that was a really good description, because, hey, that's Chicago.

That's what Chicago is about. Ethnic people keep pushing that rock up that hill every single day, trying to get a better job, trying to get a better house, trying to get a better education for their kids, trying to pay their bills—simple things like that. That's what that is: the sustained pushing of the rock up the hill. That's Chicago and Pittsburgh. That's the connection, and I think Mike Ditka feels that right down to his very soul.

Ditka's father was a steel mill guy, a very tough guy—the kind of guy who had a little union off to the side that dealt with the train transport. Those steel mill towns in Pennsylvania are like castles—there is one big, long bridge that goes into the steel mill, and the whole town is built around it. Mike Ditka Sr., and about thirty guys held off about six thousand people when they went on strike. They blocked the bridge with axe handles and wouldn't let anyone through until they made their point.

When I was in Pittsburgh I talked to a couple of guys, like the guy who was driving the shuttle, and asked them, "What do you think of Mike Ditka?" "Mike Ditka's the greatest; his family's the greatest," they would say. The guy driving the shuttle started telling me stories about his father or grandfather having the locker next to Mike Ditka's dad. He just kept saying what wonderful people they are, and how they retired in Aliquippa when they could have gone anywhere. They retired to the hill on top of Aliquippa where all the steel workers retired.

Ditka goes back to Aliquippa every year, holds a golf tournament, and supports the football team. The whole community has basically changed now, but he supports the team and the city. If you ask people in Aliquippa what they think of Mike Ditka, they will tell you he is the greatest.

I had become a big fan of Mike Ditka, and like all of Chicago, I was thrilled when the Bears won the 1985 Super Bowl championship. A few years later, I began to follow Mike Ditka's career. I thought to myself, "This guy is a very interesting person." I decided I wanted to go back through old newspapers to find out if Mike Ditka was consistent from day one—from January 20, 1982, when he became the Bears' coach—and throughout his career with the Bears.

Not only did I find that Ditka was consistent, I also found a whole universe of wonderful things about him. I discovered that he was intelligent, witty, and the most intense competitor—all these great things came out of my research. When I came home from work, I would go through the papers or go to the library and look up quotes about Mike Ditka. I realized that he was a totally unique person. The man was just incredible. I began to find a lot of little threads in Mike Ditka's personality.

One of those was his loyalty to the Bears organization. That basically occurred because George Halas took a chance and named an assistant coach at Dallas to be the head coach of the Bears. Mike Ditka came out of nowhere. When he was hired, everybody in the Chicago media said, "Mike Ditka? You've got to be kidding me. Who is he?" Mike Ditka said, "In three years, we're going to be at the Super Bowl." And everybody laughed at him. They said, "He's off his rocker; there's no way this collection of Bears is ever going to do anything." Of course, they won the Super Bowl in 1985, and the rest is history.

There are some myths about why George Halas picked Ditka, because when Halas introduced him to the press, he said, "I've been working on this plan for several years. This plan is now complete with the hiring of Mike Ditka." Well, that's not exactly the way it happened.

The Thanksgiving before Halas hired Ditka in January, he saw Ditka on television with the Cowboys, and he saw him throw his clipboard into the stands. According to one of the members of the team who was with him at the time, Halas said, "That's him, that's my coach." So there was no long-range plan.

I also found out that Mike Ditka came cheap, which for George Halas was really important. Halas didn't pay him much, and Ditka said, "Well, I don't really care what he's paying me, because if I win it's not going to matter, and if I lose it's not going to matter." So Ditka knew exactly what he was getting into.

> Q: What consumer product is named after a school's mascot?
> A: Gatorade. It was developed by a professor at the University of Florida under a grant from the Stokely-Van Camp Co.

I ended up collecting about four thousand quotes covering 1982 to 1987, and I thought that I had enough material for a book. I thought that other Bears fans might enjoy reading it, and if they didn't, I'd have something I could keep and refer to. It turned out to be highly entertaining, and there was a lot of insight into the Bears personalities at the time—people like Jim McMahon and the Fridge. There was a lot of really good stuff in the book.

I looked at publishers in Chicago and mailed a draft out to six of them. Three actually called me back, which really surprised me. Chicago Review Press liked it, and they picked it up. They wanted to know if Mike Ditka had approved of the book or knew anything about it. When I said "no," they asked me to send a draft of the book to him and get something in writing from him saying that he liked the book or the concept. I didn't think there was any way he was going to do that. But I called his secretary, Mary Albright, explained who I was, and told her that I wanted to send Coach Ditka a copy of the book to see if he liked it. She said, "Okay, no problem."

I later found out that she is Mike Ditka's agent, and has been for many years, which says a lot about the man. A man whose secretary is also his agent—in this day and age, that's really fantastic. I sent the manuscript to him and called her a couple of times and couldn't get through. Finally I got through to her, and I asked if Ditka liked the book. She said, "Let me put it to you this way. He comes in at about 5:00 in the morning and I heard him back in his office laughing hysterically." I asked her if he would mind sending a little letter saying he liked the book. I thought it was really an imposition at the time, but, true to form, Mike Ditka actually sent me a letter congratulating me on the book and wishing me well on the project. He doesn't know who I am. I'm not a professional author. For Mike Ditka to do that for somebody as insignificant as me in the whole scheme of things—that just really floored me. But Mike Ditka does that for people.

It was exciting to walk into a bookstore and see my name on books. I did a couple of radio shows, and I did one with Wally Phillips, who was like an icon in Chicago. I was totally impressed with Wally Phillips because he actually read the book before he interviewed me. He loved the book and as a result of that a lot of people read it. I've never heard anything negative said about it.

That's because they get the total picture of Mike Ditka; they get the funny Mike Ditka, the young Mike Ditka, the competitive Mike Ditka, the creative Mike Ditka—they get the full picture. It really made me feel good to know that people weren't getting just one side of him, like "da Coach," some kind of media creation; they got to see the whole man.

They said, "He's off his rocker; there's no way this collection of Bears is ever going to do anything."

This is a man who makes mistakes and admits he makes mistakes. He was arrested for drunk driving and was very apologetic about it. He gets mad at people in the media, at fans—it's all right there in the book. Like Mike Ditka says, "Why should I be anything else than who I am? This is me. Take it or leave it."

He is just a total up-front, honest personality, and this is what I love about the guy. But because he is that way, people are always trying to take cheap shots at him. He got some cheap shots from columnists in Chicago toward the end of his career, and he definitely got some cheap shots from Armen Keteyian, who wrote *Monster of the Midway*. That stuff really bothers him and it bothers me too, because it's not accurate.

People don't realize that Ditka was operating with one hand tied behind his back a lot of the time he was in Chicago. He had a big problem with Mike McCaskey. When you go through the book, you can see the threads of the problem. You can see when things started happening. First, Jim McMahon had a problem in his rear, so he went to an acupuncturist. Mike McCaskey, behind the scenes—and even out front to the media—made a big deal about it, saying, "Why is the coach stepping into this?" It was almost like he was saying, "If they lose, it's because Ditka allowed an acupuncturist to treat McMahon's butt." Of course, Jim McMahon really reamed out McCaskey, and I don't think it sat very well with him. Right after they won the Super Bowl, Wilber Marshall got away to the Redskins.

Then the real crusher came in '86, when McCaskey fired Jerry Vainisi, Ditka's closest friend in football. And then after that there was the problem with the strike. That kind of stuff created real problems. Then there was the Jim Harbaugh quarterback pick, which Mike Ditka knew nothing about. They made some bad drafts that I don't think Ditka was involved in, but it was still on Ditka's record. He had all that stuff against him.

But Mike Ditka will always be loyal to the Bears organization. The Halas/McCaskey family had to take McCaskey out of his job as CEO for the Bears because he screwed up the team, but Mike didn't criticize or say anything about him. Then they let Mike Ditka get away, and I think a lot of Chicagoans wanted to lynch them for that.

I lived in Chicago until 1988, when I got a job in North Miami. In 1995, one of my friends told me that Ditka was going to be doing a heart unit dedication at Baptist Hospital in Miami, and thought I should go down to see him. So I grabbed a couple of my books and went down there. They had a big tent set up. Mike limped up to the stage, because his hip is so bad, and gave a very stirring talk. Mike Ditka is a big guy on quotes, and he was quoting Abraham Lincoln in his speech. He gave a tremendous talk about modern-day athletes, Abraham Lincoln, and what's important in life—really inspirational words.

Afterward, he took a couple of questions. I raised my hand and he picked me right away. I said, "Coach Ditka, I'm your greatest fan." Then I asked him a two-part question that I thought would allow him to expound on his football philosophy. The second part was "Would you ever consider coaching the Dolphins?" Everybody laughed when I said that. The first part was: "When you first took over the Bears on January 20, 1982, you talked about having ACEs, which is an acronym for attitude, character, and enthusiasm. Would you describe what you meant by that?" He went off on that for a while. He was smiling when he answered the second part. He was very diplomatic. He said, "Well, Coach Shula (the Dolphins coach at the time) can coach as long as he wants, but if he ever leaves, I might be interested and someone can talk to me." It was kind of a noncommittal answer, but that's when I knew he was coming back to football. There was no question about it.

Then he had a little autograph signing. I brought my books up to him and said, "Coach Ditka, I don't know if you remember me—" And he said, "Of course I remember you." I don't know if he did or not, but it was a great thing to say.

Yvonne Davis is married to 1946 Heisman winner Glenn Davis. Before that she was married to the 1954 Heisman winner, the late Alan Ameche.

photo courtesy of Harry Caray's Restaurant

GO TO DITKA'S
GRANT DePORTER

Grant DePorter is the managing partner of Harry Caray's Restaurant in Chicago. When Harry Caray's opened in late 1987, Ditka's City Lights was the most popular nightspot in the Windy City. The menu at Caray's under "Pork Chops" said, "Go to Ditka's."

I think part of the reason Harry Caray's existed is because Ditka was around, and Harry liked to see what Mike was doing. So when Harry was approached about doing his own restaurant, he already knew about Ditka's. They were friends; they liked each other. Harry would eat at Ditka's. We were an Italian steakhouse, and that first year we had a plain pork chop on the menu, which was what Ditka's was known for. We didn't do it after that first year.

Mike has eaten here many times and has always been great. Mike always liked Harry because he was a big St. Louis Cardinals baseball fan when he was growing up in Pennsylvania. Stan Musial, the great Cardinal, was from Donora, Pennsylvania, near where Ditka was raised, and Ditka used to listen to the Cardinals' night games on KMOX in St. Louis, where Harry broadcast from 1945 to 1969.

> **Part of the reason Harry Caray's existed is because Ditka was around, and Harry liked to see what Mike was doing.**

Two of the greatest quarterbacks of all time, Johnny Unitas and Dan Marino, have the same middle name—Constantine.

photo courtesy of *Dallas Cowboys Weekly*

THE AVERAGE CHICAGOAN
BUTCH McGUIRE

Butch McGuire has owned Butch McGuire Saloon, a Chicago institution, for more than forty years.

I knew Mike when he was a Bears football player. The Bears used to frequent us on Monday afternoons at about 2:00 or 3:00 P.M. We were usually very happy to see them leave at about 5:00 or 5:30. From our place, they would go to Pat Herrons'.

You can't even get near Ditka. The downside of having professional athletes as customers is the jock sniffers that come around when they're there. That is the problem—it's not the athletes themselves. I don't know about the new, modern athletes. I think they really have a lot of problems. But Ditka and his fellow players were all good guys.

Mike represents the average Chicagoan.

The Green Bay guys used to hang around our saloon whenever they were in town. A lot of them came here when they weren't playing. The group that was with Paul Hornung was different. Paul still comes in when he is in town. Today's professional athlete, in my estimation, is nothing but a rich bum, with rare exceptions. The great ones, like Singletary, who is a wonderful, intelligent gentleman—you never saw his face. Chasing broads and hanging around saloons—that just wasn't his game.

Mike represents the average Chicagoan. He was a hardworking son of an immigrant who was successful in high school and college athletics and went on to become a very well-known professional athlete. His teammates loved him. Halas loved him. He was their leader. The guys would get out of line, and he would whip them back in line. He was good for the Bears, and the Bears were obviously good for him. I think everybody still wishes he coached the Bears. The McCaskey kid was the fly in the ointment. Ditka had a fine organization and McCaskey just decided to break it up. He wouldn't let Ditka draft whom he wanted. It was a horror show for Ditka; it was just tragic.

The average NFL salary is more than $800,000.

Mike Ditka

HE HATES TO LOSE
DAN REEVES

Dan Reeves played with the Cowboys for eight years and has been Ditka's buddy since they were teammates in 1968. After serving as Tom Landry's assistant in Dallas, Reeves went on to coach the Denver Broncos, the New York Giants, and the Atlanta Falcons, where he is today.

We were playing gin rummy one night in 1968, and after Ditka lost a couple of hands he picked up a chair and threw it across the room. All four legs stuck in the wall. All I could say was, "God, this guy hates to lose."

THE KILLER INSTINCT
CHET COPPOCK

photo courtesy of WMAQ 670AM

Chet Coppock is arguably the best sports talk radio host in America.

There is no one I've ever had greater admiration for than George Halas. I recall telling him that I thought Ditka was a logical choice for the Bears' coach because the ball club for so long had lacked anything resembling a killer instinct. There were Fencik and Plank and a handful of other guys, but as a collective unit there was no energy in the ball club. It was a very indifferent football team.

Then Ditka arrived. I called the old man the night before he arrived, and George was like a kid under the Christmas tree. He kept talking about how wonderful it was to have Mike Ditka come back to Chicago. I remember the press conference that took place in Halas's office. There were so many reporters and cameramen, they were actually standing on top of Halas's desk. Rudy Custer, who was George's business manager, was telling the cameramen to "get the hell off of the desk." By contrast, when Abe Gibron took over the ball club in 1972, there couldn't have been more than a dozen people at his press conference. It really wasn't a press conference so much as a shouting match between Mugs Halas and Bill Gleason about how the Bears were being covered.

I had the good fortune to be with Ditka and Mike Pyle up in Ditka's suite the night before the Bears played New England in Super Bowl

XX. That was not their big game that year; the big game was when they knocked off the Giants in the first round of the playoffs. When they shut out Parcells, put Joe Morris under wraps, took Phil Simms completely out of his element, and blanked the Giants, that, for all practical purposes, was when the Chicago Bears were crowned the National Football League champions.

The point at which the club really began to emerge was in 1984, when they beat the Raiders. During that game, you knew you were looking at something very, very special. Now, I have seen the team play some physical football games. In 1968, when Sayers ran for 205 yards in Green Bay, there was absolutely nothing short of manslaughter going on between the two ball clubs. But after that 1984 game against the Raiders, I remember Merlin Olsen, who worked that ballgame for NBC with Dickie Enberg, saying that he had never seen a more violent football game.

When I was with Mike the night before the Super Bowl in 1986, and we were doing his radio show on WMAQ radio, I remember this remarkable aura of tranquility permeating Ditka's suite. There was no feeling of impending confrontation. There was no feeling that the next day was a mission from God, or that Armstrong was going to land on the moon. He appeared to have a very cut-and-dried attitude about the whole thing.

I always got a kick out of the way Ditka operated on his show. Here's this guy from Aliquippa, Pennsylvania, who has a lot of savvy. It used to kill me to watch him do his radio show. He would put one half of the headset up to his ear, and he would sit there and watch television. But he was still so adept at answering questions and maintaining the flow of the show.

> Joe Klecko is only player to be All-NFL
> at three positions.

Ditka's just a very gifted guy. There isn't a doubt in my mind that if Ditka had wanted to be a broadcaster, he could have been one in the conventional sense, and not just a studio host. He could have been a sportscaster in the classic sense of the word. When I finally began to take him on, in 1992 when the ball club was playing badly, I felt like Mike had run his course. It was very difficult for me to suggest that it was time for Ditka to step down.

For a long time after that, Mike and I really didn't speak to each other. Finally, sometime in 1995, one of my local friends said, "You know, Ditka and you had a pretty good friendship. Why don't you contact him and at least try to reopen the friendship?" So I wrote Mike a letter. It was not a syrupy apology letter; it was just a letter in which I said, "I hope you know I respect you and think you're a hell of a guy. The Hall of Fame waited much too long to put you in." He wrote me back this very simple letter, but I've never forgotten how beautiful it was in its simplicity: "I don't hold grudges. You remain one of my friends. God bless you. Mike Ditka."

I'm not sure if Mike Ditka has ever found complete happiness.

That meant a lot to me, because I think we tend to look at him and see this larger-than-life, complex figure who's just a series of contradictions.

Another great story about Mike takes place during his first year back in Chicago. He hadn't yet coached a ballgame. There was a charity golf tournament for NFL alumni in the summer of 1982, and I was emceeing it out at Beverly Golf Club. Former Bears great Eddie Sprinkle was in charge of the tournament; he was one of the sweetest guys in the world. I thought that with Ditka being back in town as the new head coach with a new regime, it would be great to have Mike speak to the crowd. I asked him, "Mike, do you mind doing ten minutes?" "Oh sure," he said. "No problem."

So the banquet started rolling—but no Ditka. Dinner was served—still no Ditka. I walked up to one of his assistant coaches and said, "Where's Mike?" "I have no idea," he said. So I walked downstairs to the locker room. And there was Mike, playing cards with Reggie Fleming. I said, "Coach, we need you in about twenty minutes. Can you walk up?"

After twenty minutes, there was still no Ditka. I called up Earl Morrall, the former Lion, to speak. I called up Jimmie Taylor. Then I sneaked down to the locker room to get Ditka. He was lying against the locker, completely asleep. Well, not asleep—he was drunk.

A GREAT COACH

Ditka's unpredictability factor is so unreal. Who in the world trades the entire store for a running back? Only Ditka would have the rocks to do something like that.

The young Mike Ditka used to hang out at Chicago Stadium and was nuts about the Blackhawks. He used to sit in the front row at the turn behind the glass. He was a huge hockey fan. He was nuts about Bobby Hull and Stan Mikita. He was everything a man's man was supposed to be.

There is a part of Mike Ditka that Mike Ditka will never sell. And there's a part of Mike Ditka that leaves him something less than

In order to host the Pro Bowl from 1994 to 1998, the state of Hawaii had to donate the use of the stadium and guarantee the NFL $1 million income each year.

fully complete. Mike will have friendships that are absolutely locked in stone, and something will go wrong and he just won't be able to leverage them back into a rightful position. In Mike's case, it's almost like he thinks that his masculinity would be threatened if he were to do that. It's very unfortunate.

I'm not sure if Mike Ditka has ever found complete happiness. I'll give you a great story about Mike. The

> **I think in his own mind, Mike feels that there is a group of people who refuse to recognize him as a so-called "great coach."**

Bears danced on Ray Berry's face at the Super Bowl. The ballgame was over twenty seconds after the coin toss. The next day, I was hosting the Ditka show on WMAQ out of the studios at the Merchandise Mart. My first question was something about winning the ballgame. It was obvious that Mike was very relaxed. The first thing he said to me was "They're lucky we didn't score sixty points on them." He said it with a very sardonic and sarcastic feel to his voice, but you got the sense that maybe he felt that people hadn't paid enough homage to the Bears, or to him.

I don't think Mike would admit that he battles to this day for the respect of former 49ers coach Bill Walsh. That is why Mike has very derisively called him a genius. I think in his own mind, Mike feels that there is a group of people who refuse to recognize him as a so-called "great coach." I absolutely do. But I think there is a part of Mike that has always sought a certain kind of parental approval, especially since he and his father were not particularly close. I don't think Mike has to prove a damn thing to anybody.

ONE TAKE EACH

I was waxed at Channel 5 in November of 1983. It came out of nowhere. I was making a lot of money—I had more than a million dollars of contract money. So I was fighting for a settlement. My wife was pregnant; my life was up in the air—the whole nine yards.

Lo and behold, as a part of the settlement, I wound up at WMAQ radio as the sports director. I was going to launch a brand new vehicle—not a sports talk show, but a sports magazine format in which I would have four or five live guests per night. I asked Mike if he would come down to the studio and cut a couple of promos for me.

As it happened, about a week later, Mike and I were both appearing at a banquet. He was the principal speaker and I was the emcee. I said, "Why don't you stop by afterward?" I told him not to park at the Merchandise Mart because it was inside. But he got confused and had to park outside the Mart.

Now, he had just had significant surgery, and he was on crutches. The windchill factor was about twenty-five below, and he was only wearing a sports coat. The poor guy walked over on crutches.

By the time he got there, he was absolutely crimson. I thought, "My God, do I call a paramedic and have him treated for frostbite?" It was 8:00. I had a tape recorder and I turned it on. I told Mike, "You have about twenty-eight and one-half seconds, so let's talk about you." I knew he was frozen to death, he hurt like hell, and he didn't want to be there, but he did two spots—one take each. One take each! No one does that, not even experienced old pros. But Ditka did.

DON'T SAY NO TO HIM

Everyone knows about Mike's inability to separate the various components of his relationships. I think there's a part of Mike that has that old-fashioned, western Pennsylvania mentality. Part of it is defiance, and part of it is trying to please a father figure that he felt was never quite pleased by him.

The great thing about Jerry Vainisi, who was the Bears' general manager when Ditka was coach, was that on the days Mike was pissed off, Jerry would go back and pour him a scotch on the rocks. He

Don't you ever say no to this guy.

was a shoulder for Mike to lean on. There were times, in my opinion, when Vainisi may have saved Ditka from self-destruction. Of course, now they aren't nearly as close as they once were.

Another example is Steve Kasor, who was Ditka's special teams coach in Chicago for the entire run. He told me that he couldn't even get a call in to Ditka about getting a job with the New Orleans Saints. Kasor feels terribly left out by Ditka. He's not the only one.

Ditka reminds me a lot of Bobby Knight. I played golf one day with Bobby and Doc, the Indiana team doctor and a local fixture in Bloomington, and Sam Carmichael, who owned a beautiful course between Bloomington and Indianapolis. We played golf, wrapped up the round, hung around for a while, and then our wives joined us.

My wife Nancy, Doc's wife, and Sam Carmichael's wife all drove up to meet us. We were all going to have dinner together that night. Then Knight said, "All right, you guys all go home, Coppock's going to ride with me."

So I rode with Bobby. We got back to the university, and boom! What happens? We sat there talking for an hour, then two hours, and then we finally got showered. Three hours had gone by, and we didn't get to the restaurant until 9:30. Everybody else was there by 6:00.

We walked in, and Nancy didn't say a word. Nobody said a word. They were all too afraid. I was even tempted to say, "Bobby, for

God's sake, we've got to get the hell out of here." But you just don't do that with a guy like Bobby.

There are those people in life who people strive to be close to, and as a result will put up with any number of idiosyncrasies that are either particular, or spoiled, or just screwed up. Ditka and Bobby Knight both fall into that category. I think Lombardi probably fell into that category, and Auerbach, too. The list goes on and on.

One thing you have to remember about Ditka: Don't you ever say no to this guy. Don't you ever suggest that he can't do something, because he'll ram it right down your throat.

AN IMPOSING FIGURE

Ditka got in a fight in the first game he ever played, on September 13, 1961. It was the Vikings' first game in Minneapolis, and the Bears got creamed by Tarkenton, who was a rookie for the Vikings. Norm Van Brocklin, the Dutchman, was the Vikings' head coach.

Ditka hauled off and slugged one of his own teammates, Ted Karras, Alex Karras's brother. Ditka apparently was upset about the way Karras was playing. He was furious that the Bears got trampled in their opener, so he hauled off and took a swing at his teammate.

With the sponsors, Ditka was tremendous—when he wanted to be. That was part of Ditka's unpredictability factor, and you either had to learn to accept it or you had to walk away from it. A lot of the players could not deal with it. The bulk of the press, whether they would admit it or not, were absolutely scared to death of Ditka.

After all, he was such an imposing figure and an enormous physical specimen. The guy was a combination of Hulk Hogan and Sonny Liston.

Jim Thorpe was the first president of the NFL.

DITKA, THE WRITE WAY
DON PIERSON

Don Pierson writes for the Chicago Tribune *and is the author of* Ditka: An Autobiography, *which was published in 1986.*

I was covering the Bears for the *Tribune* and a publisher called up and asked if we would be interested in writing a book about Ditka. We weren't, but he talked us into it, and I'm glad we did it.

During the writing of the book, Ditka was terrific—very accessible. We worked out a deal: I would come to his home at a certain time and if it wasn't convenient, we would do it when it was. We weren't going to make this a pain in the ass; we were going to have fun doing it. He was always very professional about it and I don't think he ever changed the schedule. We must have talked for thirty or thirty-five hours.

That '85 season was great, and every win would have helped us sell the book, but the publisher didn't care whether the Bears won or not after they sold enough books to pay us off. It should have gone coast to coast, but they didn't care about distribution at all. You couldn't get that book. McMahon's book sold 300,000 copies. Ditka was always mad about that—that McMahon sold more books than he did.

LOOK WHO'S COMING TO DINNER
KEITH BUCHERT

Keith Buchert owns the Timbers Supper Club in Platteville, Wisconsin, where the Chicago Bears have trained every summer since 1984.

Mike Ditka dined here frequently. Prior to the breakup of camp, he would bring all his coaches in for dinner. He always left every server a hundred-dollar tip—he was just a great guy and a good customer.

Once, Refrigerator Perry and Steve McMichael came in. They were sitting in the bar having cocktails. At the time, Ditka was putting the heat on Perry to lose weight. Perry and McMichael ordered an appetizer tray, and Perry made a stick man out of the carrots and celery and bribed one of the waiters to take it over to Ditka's table.

Another time, after they won the Super Bowl, he was sitting in the lounge, which was full of people. Somebody said, "Mike, what does that Super Bowl ring look like?" So he took it off and passed it around the bar so everybody could look at it. I thought that was nice.

He was always very gracious and never forgot who his fans were. He was never offended by anyone asking for an autograph. One time a woman saw him here, and she pointed and said, "Oh my gosh, it's Mike Ditka." He happened to see that, and he walked over to her table and gave her a little kiss. She thought that was just great.

He always left every server a hundred-dollar tip.

After Ditka left, attendance kind of went down.

I ran into him at the restaurant show in Chicago and we talked. I said, "We really miss you at the Timbers." We were at the ESPN booth, and they were taking pictures. He signed one "Good luck to all of you at the Timbers." He said he'd had some great times at the Timbers and remembered us well.

Kansas City's Arrowhead Stadium was the first stadium designed exclusively for football. It opened in 1972 next door to Royals Stadium.

A NEIGHBORHOOD KIND OF GUY
TOM DREESEN

A native of the Chicago sub-urbs, comedian Tom Dreesen was Frank Sinatra's opening act for thirteen years. He's a member of a celebrity golf tour and often plays with Mike Ditka.

itka was so popular in Chicago for the same reasons Harry Caray was popular in Chicago. Chicagoans are different from the residents of most other cities because they live in such a blue-collar town. Harry reminded you of a bartender in the corner tavern. Mike reminds you of a guy who would have a bar called "Iron Mike's"—he's a neighborhood kind of guy.

Ditka, no matter what he does, no matter what he accomplishes, no matter where he goes, will always be the kind of guy neighborhood guys feel they can approach. And they do, by the way. They walk up to him all the time in bars.

But when they look Ditka in the eye, they also know they can't give him a ration of shit. If they give Ditka shit he'll look at them with the coldest eyes you've ever seen in your life. He can freeze you right in your spot.

I've seen him do that to football teams. I've seen him go in at halftime and blow the roof off the locker room. And I've heard him tell his players, "When you get your check, back up to get it, because you sure as hell didn't earn it today."

I thought Ditka would be a good coach for the Bears because he was what they needed at the time, and he had a bundle of talent. Now those Bears days are gone, and I wonder how he'll do in New Orleans. There are prima donnas in football today; they play for the money and not for the game. It's all special teams now—this guy coaches the defense, that guy coaches the quarterbacks, this guy coaches the downtrodden and the meek.

Mike is an intense coach; it's his way or the highway. But as tough and as strong as Mike Ditka is, he is very gentle when he sees a child, and certainly if he sees a disabled child. He just melts. As strong as he is, he's also very compassionate and very sensitive to other people.

He can freeze you right in your spot.

Mike's about a five-handicap golfer—extremely intense. One time he missed a lob shot on the side of the green, and he promptly left the green, took a sand wedge, and beat it against the side of a tree until it shattered. Either the tree or the sand wedge was going to go, and it turned out it was the sand wedge.

Mike calls me to do shows since I am a master of ceremonies. I have done so many of those things, and Mike was on the dais with me at the Harry Caray roast, so when the time came, Mike wanted me to be the master of ceremonies for his charity.

I've stayed in his home on the North Side of Chicago. His wife Diana is perfect for him. She's a southern gal who adores him. That's her man. She allows him the freedom to be himself. You can't throw a harness around a guy like Ditka. If you do, he'll just drag you along like a mule plowing the fields.

When Mike Ditka was playing and he got the football, he wasn't the fastest guy in the world, but it took two trucks to bring him down.

If Mike Ditka ran for office, he could have done just what Jesse Ventura did.

When he got the ball, he simply did not want to be tackled. Sometimes it would take half the team to bring him down. His legs would still be pumping. That's the kind of football player he was, and that's the kind of person he is. He's a straight ahead, dig in, put your head in, and go for it kind of guy.

Mike is up in years now, but I have seen people come up to him in Iron Mike's and want his autograph. Some people are really nice, and then there are those guys with the big beer bellies and crew cuts who you know are just looking for some shit. They're just looking to argue with him so they can go home and tell everybody they got into it with Ditka. But the way Mike looks at them, and the way he answers them, they know immediately they've got the wrong guy.

In a neighborhood, it's almost like a fort. In the old days, the pioneers in the wilderness carved out a fort to protect themselves from the elements. The neighborhood tavern is like that; it's where everybody goes.

Chicago was a city of boundaries for many, many years. The Irish took over here. The Polish took over there. The Italians took over there. The blacks took over there. There were neighborhoods. When you got inside your neighborhood, there was a comfort there, a safety.

The people who stood out the most in those neighborhoods were those who told the truth. If they said they would be there at 9:00, they were there at 9:00. If they said they were going to help you move at 9:00 on Saturday morning, and even if they were out drinking until 5:00 in the morning, they still had to be there at 9:00 because you're only as good as your word. All my life I've told my children: you're judged by two things—your work and your word. If this is your work, whatever it is, do it the best that you can. If this is your word, never, ever go back on it.

Mike Ditka exemplifies all that. His work ethic cannot be denied, nor can his word. Mike is the kind of guy who, right or wrong, tells it like it is. That's why he was such a big hit on NBC. I was with him just before he took the coaching job in New Orleans, and I thought he was crazy for taking it, because we loved to hear what he would say on the air. For instance, a young football quarterback would be doing this or that and would be holding out. One of the coaches would say, "Well, you've got to talk to him and get hold of his agent." Mike would say, "What he needs is a good slap in the face." And everybody would say, "Yeah, that's exactly what he needs." Mike said that about that quarterback, Jeff George, who gave everybody so many problems everywhere he went. Mike said it on national television. Everybody in every bar in every city said, "Yeah." Because he speaks like us. That's the way you talk in the neighborhoods. Mike doesn't pull any punches. He doesn't speak out of both sides of his mouth.

Today, in a time when voter apathy is up, young people have no respect whatsoever for anyone who runs for office. Why did Jesse Ventura, a wrestler, become a governor? If Mike Ditka ran for office, he could have done just what Jesse Ventura did. Common people would have voted for him because he told it like it was.

> Pat Riley never played college football but was drafted by the Dallas Cowboys. His brother, Lee, played seven years in the NFL.

photo courtesy of *Dallas Cowboys Weekly*

DRESSED TO IMPRESS
PALMER PYLE

Brother of Mike Pyle, Palmer had a stellar high school career in suburban Chicago and starred at Michigan State. After a successful pro career with the Eagles and the Raiders, Palmer became a radio executive in Phoenix, Las Vegas, Jacksonville, and Michigan.

On Tuesdays, we'd all go out and hit the town after practice. Every Wednesday, Mike would come to practice in a suit so he could go right back to the same places to apologize. I remember that vividly.

DA BEARS
ROBERT SMIGEL

In the early 1990s, the "Saturday Night Live" cast started per-forming a skit entitled "Sports Fans." Robert Smigel was the key player in that scenario, which allowed such phrases as "da Coach," "da Bears," and "da Bulls," to become part of America's lingo.

I grew up in New York, but I lived in Chicago in the early '80s. I was there taking improv classes. I'm a huge sports fan. I always thought New York was the be-all and end-all, but when I went to Chicago I could see it was a better sports town than any town I'd ever seen. The fans were so devoted and so hilarious, because with devotion often comes insanity. There was a crazy element to the fans—how they took stuff seriously but often with good humor.

That's when I really started noticing the look that a lot of Chicago fans have. It was the beefiness that naturally accumulates from years of sausage eating and beer drinking, the proud, oversized avi-ator shades that had gone out of style about five years earlier, and the thick mustache, which was very Ditka-like. So I started making fun of the fans and their cocky attitudes.

That's what led to the sketch that Bob Odenkirk and I came up with for "Saturday Night Live." I actually performed the sketch in Chicago before we were both writers for SNL five years later.

Suddenly, "da Bears" and "da Bulls" became catchphrases in Chicago. In the script I didn't even spell it "da," I just wrote " the" and we pronounced it "da." I didn't know it was going be a catch-phrase. Then we did the sketch again when George Wendt came on

The holy trinity was basically God, Ditka, and Halas.

the show, and I started seeing these banners at Bulls games on ESPN that said "da Bulls." Then the Bulls started inviting us to their championship celebrations. I realized that this had turned into something.

Ditka was just a natural extension of the sketch. The fans would elevate the Bears to this godlike status, and the holy trinity was basically God, Ditka, and Halas. We did one bit speculating on the seating arrangements up in heaven—there's God, then there's Halas and Jesus and Brian Piccolo.

Ditka has such a quintessential Chicago look that he became the role model for our characters—he embodied everything that was masculine and proper and good on the planet. The characters would rhapsodize about his hair and how sharp it was, and his brain—they'd say that when the coach passes, at least science will have the benefit of examining his brain. The mother lode of information that would come forth would be blinding. It's a complex network of nerve endings covered with a very sharp haircut.

We did the sketch eight times on "Saturday Night" over a period of about five years. It was like a brush fire. It started as "da Bears," then it became "da Bulls," and then it became a national thing. Then it sort of got embraced by rap music. It first began with us making fun of these white guys with Chicago accents.

It took on a life of its own in ways that I didn't ever envision. Jim Downey, the producer at the time, says it's the most repeated catchphrase of any catchphrase that was manufactured on SNL. There are catchphrases that people have said in real life that then become famous on SNL. This was something that just came out of nothing, and he thought it was the most ubiquitous manufactured catchphrase in the show's history.

I named the characters Super Fans because I remembered a guy in Chicago who went to Cubs games and wore a super hero costume. He called himself "Super Fan." This was in the early '80s. I thought, "That's what these guys would call themselves on their radio show."

Joe Mantegna was Bill Swerski, and when George Wendt hosted the next time we did it we made him Bob Swerski, Bill's brother. From then on Bob always did it because Bill was out recovering from another heart attack; he was always recovering from heart attacks. We named them after Chuck Swersky, a sportscaster in Chicago. Bob Odenkirk picked the name Swerski. We spelled it with an "i" instead of with a "y." Chris Farley was Todd O'Connor. Mike Meyers was in the sketch, too. His character's name was Pat Arnold. My character's name was Carl Wollarski.

I don't usually perform on SNL, but Jim Downey placed me in the sketch because he was from Joliet, near Chicago, and he didn't feel like anybody else was doing the accent as well. So he wanted me in there. He used to call me the metronome for the sketch because if I did a few lines with a perfect accent the whole sketch would sound a little better in his mind.

He actually felt like I did the accent better than George Wendt, who grew up on the South Side of Chicago. Farley grew up in Madison, Wisconsin. Mike Meyers grew up in Canada, so he was at a disadvantage, too. But for some reason, I had a natural affinity for "dat particular accent as per Jim Downey's ear."

> Greasy Neale is the only person to play in a World Series, coach a Rose Bowl team, and coach an NFL champion.

I always thought that no one would get the joke outside of Chicago. After that first season, we only did it twice. It was a phenomenon in Chicago because it coincided with the Bulls winning their first championship, so everything magnified intensely because of all the excitement. Then we were invited to do a comic relief tribute to Michael Jordan the summer after they won the championship. Michael Jordan participated in a sketch on the stage of the Chicago Theater and we had a blast. Then we were invited to do a Bears thing at the Super Bowl. We did all these crazy things over the years.

We actually stepped onto the field before a Bears playoff game in December 1991, when they played the Cowboys. The three of us— George Wendt, Chris Farley, and I— went out to the middle of the field and they introduced us. Then at halftime we participated in the field goal competition for the kids. Farley went first; he took a huge fall and rolled around in the mud and got a huge laugh. I was next and I thought, "There's no way I can top Farley comedically, so I'm actually going to try to kick the ball through." But I had to do it in a funny way, so I held my beer as I did it. I kicked a field goal with a crappy little sneaker. I just managed to kick a twenty yarder and I got a huge cheer. Then I cockily held up my beer and took the applause. It was surreal. George Wendt went last, and he had a great way to finish it off. He called an audible and had me hike the ball to him, and Farley lined up on defense. I threw a block on Farley and George ran in for a touchdown. It was the dumbest thing ever, and it got the biggest cheer. It was completely moronic.

After Ditka was fired, we brought the characters back and they wrote a letter of protest to Michael McCaskey. The whole sketch

> In the 1931 Rose Bowl, "Five Yards" Fogarty carried the ball twenty-five times and gained exactly five yards each time.

was just us sitting at a table listening while George Wendt wrote this letter of protest. We were giving back all our Bears paraphernalia—ridiculous Bears hats, underwear, a sandwich Mike Singletary had taken a bite out of that we had saved since 1986—just ridiculous souvenirs. Ditka agreed to do it, which was weird because it was the week he was fired. We had somebody go to his house in Chicago to shoot him reading the letter in his basement. On the raw footage it was pretty crappy. It was really funny because the camera guy kept wanting him to do one more take. Ditka said, "What are you talking about, how many times can I do this thing?" It was not the week to ask for extra takes.

He embodied everything that was masculine and proper and good on the planet.

We did this whole sketch where he was reading the letter, and then we dissolved to him chewing gum and reading the letter. The letter suggested that Ditka should be an astronaut, since now the only thing left for him to do was to go to the moon. He called NASA and they didn't think it was such a good idea.

He did something for us as coach of the Saints, too. We went to New Orleans and taped him in his office. He had a phone conversation with Chris Farley. In the sketch, the Super Fans were all in withdrawal because Ditka had moved to New Orleans, and we were all confused. One guy had willingly deprogrammed himself to become a Saints fan. Another guy had lost his mind and moved to the exact middle point between New Orleans and Chicago, which was a gas station in the middle of Tennessee. He had cut his uniform in half—with the Bears on one side and the Saints on the other—and he had attached the sides with nacho cheese. Farley's character was in a mental hospital because he was in denial and kept insisting it was

1986 and the Bears were 9–0. So Ditka had to talk him down and tell him to move on with his life.

Ditka was a great sport about it. I think he loved it. We used his restaurant, Ditka's City Lights, and he was thrilled because we always showed it at the beginning of the sketch. We pretended that that was where the sketch was taking place. In the opening of the sketch, we would play "Sweet Home Chicago," and there was a fake banner outside of the photo of Ditka's that said, "Every Sunday, Bob Swerski's Super Fans on WCBN Radio," or something like that. Whenever I was in Chicago I would go to Ditka's restaurant and they would treat me like a king. I would get a free meal and royal treatment.

> In 1941, Buff Donelli was the head football coach for the Pittsburgh Steelers and Duquesne University.

DITKA ON HIS BEAR DAYS

photo courtesy of Dallas Cowboys Weekly

I was tremendously proud to put on a Bears uniform. I knew very little about the Bears until I was drafted by them in 1961 because I was from Pennsylvania and mostly followed the Pittsburgh Steelers and Philadelphia Eagles. But the more I found out about the Bears, the more I liked the team; they played the kind of football that I believed in, and Coach Halas taught the kind of football I believed in. The Bears were the Monsters of the Midway, or the bullies, or whatever you want to call them, and that's the way I thought the game was supposed to be played.

I was with the College All-Stars in 1961, and we scrimmaged the Bears. I did not make any friends on the team. I ran over a couple of guys, which did not sit well with them. We played the Philadelphia Eagles, who had won the NFL title the year before. We had some very good ballplayers.

I think the first friend I made on the team was Bill George. Bill was a Pennsylvania kid from the coal mine area of western Pennsylvania. He kind of took me under his wing and helped me a little bit. And I remember Larry Morris and some of the other guys. Harlon Hill was a lot of help to me. Harlon was a great guy. It was toward the end of his career, and he spent a good amount of time working with me. He was also playing, and I think they were planning on converting him to tight end. I think they even tried him on defense because his days as a wide receiver were over, but in my day he was one of the great wide receivers.

I didn't have an agent when I came to Chicago. I don't have an agent now. I don't believe in agents. I know what I'm worth and I wouldn't fool anybody about that. My agents were myself and my dad. I was very flattered at the time to be drafted into the NFL when I was coming out of college. I didn't know if I would play in the National Football League. It was actually George Allen who signed me—he was the Bears' assistant defensive coach at the time. He said, "You know, I'm paying you more money than the Bears have paid any rookie since Red Grange," or something like that, and I knew he was lying, but still I had to laugh.

My first impression of George Halas was that he was the leader. What he said went; he was the boss, period. I saw him as being in control and very authoritative. He was the guy who got his way almost all the time, either when dealing with the Bears or the NFL.

I came to our first training camp pretty well prepared. At Pitt we worked as hard as anybody. Our coach was a stickler for hard work and tough training. Since I was used to working hard, training camp was not that difficult for me.

There was, of course, a difference from college football. At Pitt I'd played defense and blocked a lot. Catching passes was rarely on the agenda. With the Bears my job was to catch balls and block, and that was a big change for me. So when I was drafted by the Bears in '61, I went to Chicago early and worked out. That was the year

> In the 1983 Holiday Bowl, Brigham Young University quarterback Steve Young caught the winning touchdown pass in a 21–17 victory over Missouri.

the Bears traded for Bill Wade. Sid Luckman was there as an assistant coach, and he really helped me tremendously in becoming a receiver. He took the time to work with me and teach me how to catch a ball. Not that I couldn't catch the ball—I led the team at Pitt in receiving my senior year with fourteen catches or so, which tells you what our passing game was like. Sid guided me, and Bill Wade worked with me, throwing the ball to me; we just did it over and over. We worked out down at Soldier Field in those days even though we played at Wrigley Field. We worked for about three or four weeks in the summer, and it really helped me for training camp.

It was a different game then. We were all part of football as a sport, and it's not like that anymore; it's big business.

It was a different game then, too. We were all part of football as a sport, and it's not like that anymore; it's big business. We were part of pro football when it was played more for the love of the game. We played hard together on the field and off the field, and we had fun.

We were much more together as a group in those days. It was nothing for all of us to meet at a place and have a beer together or a sandwich. I think we did much more of that than the players do today.

There was also a strong camaraderie. Maybe there wasn't a great love, but there was always a great respect between our offense and defense. I always felt that. We knew that we were a team that won because of our defense, yet offensively we tried to do the things we had to do.

One of the things I did that first summer when I came to Chicago early, besides catching passes and working out, was watch a lot of game film. One day I was watching a film of the Bears playing the Lions, and I remember Joe Fortunato rushing a passer. Jim Gibbons was Detroit's tight end, and he was on the right end's side. Joe got outside of Gibbons and gave him the clothesline, took him all the way to the quarterback with him, and just dropped them both. Coach Halas happened to be in the room at the time, and he said, "Did you see that?"

I said, "Yeah, do they always do that to the tight ends?" And he said, "Not if you don't let them." I said, "Well, I'll try not to let them then." Fortunato was just a big, impressive guy and a hell of a football player.

Our finest season, of course, was 1963. The first thing I remember about that season was when we played the Giants in the preseason. We beat them, and after the game Coach Halas called me in and asked me about where I thought we could go that year. I said I thought we could win it all.

I also remember the '63 games against Green Bay, which were tremendous games. We won both (at Green Bay, 10–3, and at Wrigley Field, 26–7)—not an easy chore when they had Vince Lombardi on the sideline and players like Starr, Nitschke, Taylor, Kramer, and Davis on the field.

The game in Pittsburgh was memorable, as was the tie at the end of the year against the Vikings (which we had to get), and the game against Detroit (which we had to win), when Davey Whitsell intercepted a pass and saved the game. After all those games and the things that happened in them, the championship game against the Giants was almost anticlimactic, but it was a great game—the

Clemson University started the Booster Club concept with IPTAY (I Pay Ten a Year). Rivals claim it stands for "It's Probation Time Again, Y'all."

league's top offense (Giants) against the best defense (Bears).

The play that everybody seems to remember was in the Steelers game that year. (Ditka took a short pass and rambled sixty-three yards, shedding at least five tacklers to set up the game-tying field goal.) I don't really know that it was the best play I ever made, because if it had been the best, I would have scored a touchdown and I would have outrun that last guy. I was very tired at that point. That play was near the end of the game, and I'd played the whole game. I remember that because Wade wanted me to run a deep pattern, and I said, "No, I can't," and I told him what play to run. I said, "I'll hook up about twelve yards down, you throw me the ball, and maybe I can get across midfield." I felt that if we hit another pass or two, maybe we could score a touchdown or at least kick another field goal. Then, during my run, all those guys missed me, but I started running out of gas, and when the last guy hit me, I went down. So I wasn't going too fast. On the play after that—I had come out of the game—Wade threw a perfect pass to Bo Farrington, hit him right between the numbers in the end zone, and he dropped it. So we had to kick a field goal to tie it. When you think about the little things that made that season, it's kind of crazy. At any rate, we ended up half a game ahead of Green Bay and went out and whipped the Giants for the title.

We had some great players then. Bill George was definitely one of the all-time greatest players. There's no question in my mind about Doug Atkins, either. I don't think Dick Butkus had a peer at middle linebacker; he played the position ferociously. Bill George played it a little differently. So did Joe Schmidt of Detroit. But Butkus, Ray Nitschke of Green Bay, and Jack Lambert of Pittsburgh, they played it like: "I'm just going to kick the shit out of these guys; I've got no friends on the other side. Don't take any prisoners." I respected them for that.

There were other damn good players too: linebackers Joe Fortunato and Larry Morris, defensive end Ed O'Bradovich, tackles Fred Williams and Stan Jones. In the secondary we had Rosey Taylor, Richie Petitbon, Bennie McRae, and Davey Whitsell. So it was a very solid football team. We had J. C. Caroline backing up in the offense, and one of the game's greatest running backs and a very underrated player, Willie Galimore. I saw him after he had about five knee surgeries, but he could still fly. I never saw anybody cut and run like he could. He was very similar to Gale Sayers, but actually I thought he was faster than Gale. I don't know that he could cut as well as Gale, but they were very similar. Then, of course, we had Joe Marconi and Rick Casares at fullback, and Rudy Bukich and Bill Wade at quarterback. On the line were Bob Wetoska, Ted Karras, and Herm Lee. There was Mike Pyle at center. Bo Farrington and Johnny Morris were the wide receivers. It was a solid football team. In passing we couldn't match Baltimore's personnel, which included Johnny Unitas and Raymond Berry, but we got the job done.

Galimore and Farrington were killed at the next training camp in 1964. It was a terrible shock. You're with the guys one night, you leave a meeting with them, you have a bite to eat with them, and then it's over, forever. They went over to the country club to watch the Olympics and eat pizza. Because somebody had misplaced a road sign, they ran off the road when they were coming back, hooked a wheel, and the car flipped over. They both were killed. I

The youngest coaches in NFL history were Harlan Svare, thirty-one, 1962, Rams; David Shula, thirty-two, Bengals, 1992; John Madden, thirty-three, Raiders 1969; Don Shula, thirty-three, Colts, 1963.

can remember the shock of everyone at training camp, and it was terrible.

I played against some tough guys. Ray Nitschke of the Packers—he was as tough as they come. Willie Wood, up in Green Bay, was a really rugged defensive back; I had great respect for him. And, of course, I had to play against Herb Adderley. Another tough one was a kid out of the 49ers, Jimmy Johnson, a great defensive back. During my career, most of the trouble seemed to come from the Packers guys, like Willie

It was really something to go against the Packers in those days. There's always been a great rivalry between the Bears and Green Bay.

Davis. Another tough guy I played against was Bill Pellington, at Baltimore—he'd knock people down with his fist.

Gino Marchetti—I respected him so much. He was just a great football player. If you can block Marchetti and you can block Willie Davis, you can block anybody. Another tough one was Alex Karras from Detroit. He was pretty damn tough. There was a linebacker out of San Francisco who played in the '70s, Dave Wilcox. He played against us at the end of my Bears career, and then when I was playing at Dallas. He was a very underrated football player.

I had a couple of good run-ins with Sam Huff of the Giants, but I had great respect for Sam because he played the game the way I did. He played hard like I did, and we both felt that you can't worry about who is going to get mad at you out there as a result. If they get mad at you, they get mad at you. Sam didn't have to be big, he played so well. He wasn't small, though—I think he played linebacker at about 230 or 235 pounds.

The two best teams of my time were the Packers and the Colts. Baltimore, talent-wise, might even have been better than the Packers. They finally won the NFL championship in 1964.

It was really something to go against the Packers in those days. There's always been a great rivalry between the Bears and Green Bay. But we had a good rivalry with Baltimore, too, in those days. In fact, we had a lot of intense rivalries, including Detroit and Minnesota.

I came back to the Bears in 1982. George Halas called me. I had written him a letter some years before and had told him that if the opportunity ever arose, I would really appreciate at least talking about the possibility of coaching the Bears. And so he called me and asked if I would come in and have a talk. Actually, he didn't call me first; he called the Cowboys for permission to talk to me, and Tex Schramm, the president of the Cowboys, told me that I could. Then Halas called me at home one night and said, "Fly in and come to my apartment. Don't tell anyone about it." So that's what I did.

We sat down and talked. It was very informal, at the kitchen table. At the time, all the fair-haired guys were coming in, the new geniuses of football. I think Mr. Halas was trying to check me out to see if I was one of them, and so he asked me what my philosophy of football was. I kind of laughed and said, "You know I don't think that's important. First of all, my philosophy is the same as yours, and that's strictly to win. How we do it? We have our methods and we have our ideas. But if you're asking me if I am going to go out and throw the ball all over the ballpark like it's a wounded duck, no, I'm going to play football and teach good, basic fundamentals."

He offered me a two-year contract, but I said I wouldn't take a two-year contract; it would have to be a three-year contract, period. I said two years wasn't enough. And it wouldn't have been. He said, "Fine," and gave me the other year. It was not a very lucrative con-

tract, but it didn't matter. That was never important; the opportunity was what was important.

He gave me that opportunity, and I'm forever grateful. It's just a shame that he couldn't have stayed around to see all the good things that happened to the Bears in the 1980s. But I think he knows they happened. I think he had an inkling that they were going to happen, I really do. It's also a shame he didn't get a chance to see the '85 team, because it may have been as good a Bears team as there ever was.

In the beginning, when I first got out of playing the game, I wanted to stay with the game by coaching. I managed to do that. But I knew it would be a while before I was ready to take on a head coaching job. In fact, I never wanted to be head coach, per se. I had a good job as an assistant coach with the Dallas Cowboys, and that's a pretty secure job if you do your job. It was good because the Cowboys had won and were a very stable organization. I was working for Tom Landry and Tex Schramm, two people I loved and respected.

Everybody started talking about head coaching jobs when Dan Reeves, another of our assistants at Dallas at the time, got the Denver Broncos job.

The only job I ever wanted was the Bears job. Nobody was going to call me from New York or Atlanta or any of those kinds of teams. I was committed to the Bears' type of football—the kind George Halas had fostered. Anybody can think what they want to think or write what they want to write—it was just meant to be. That's all

> The Jacksonville Jaguars were the first major team in any sport to be completely anti-smoking in every way.

there was to it. You can call it fate, but that's how it was meant to be. I don't think anybody could have written a script with the sense of destiny I felt, beginning with my coming to Chicago in '61 and my travels and my return in '82, twenty years later.

The year 1985 was truly special. I thought we would be a pretty good football team. I thought we would be a team that would never knuckle under to anybody. I knew we were going to be tough. And then everything just came together.

We won most of the early games with offense; our defense was not sure yet. They were still getting their feet wet, and everybody had kind of picked on them. Other teams knew when we were blitzing and this and that, but once the defense cranked it up it didn't matter if they knew or not, because nobody could stop them. As the season went along, our cornerbacks got more confidence. By the end of the year, you could see from the other teams playing us that they didn't want any part of those guys, nor did they want any part of our defensive line or linebackers—Hampton, Dent, Perry, McMichael, Singletary, Marshall, and Otis Wilson. Those guys were just awfully good. And they were brutal.

We just surged to the Super Bowl, and that is the best feeling there is. Of all the feelings I've ever had, to be the head coach of a Super Bowl-winning football team is the finest, because it's a total team effort. It's nothing I did, and it's nothing any one individual on the team did; it was a collective effort by everybody in the organization from top to bottom. There were so many people to thank, even people who were gone, like Jim Finks, who had helped put the pieces in place with his excellent draft picks, and Jerry Vainisi and Bill McGrane from the front office. It was a terrific organization. It seemed like everybody worked for a common goal that year, and that's what we tried to get back. That's such a hard thing to reestablish once you have done it, because people get caught up in the whole idea of why you win or how important they were in the scheme of things instead of realizing that they were just part of the reason, and not the whole reason.

We would have made history if we would have beaten Miami in 1985, but they outcoached us. Don Shula outcoached us. They didn't outplay us—our guys were really playing hard—they just outcoached us, and I'm willing to admit that.

If we had not have lost that game, I'm not sure we would have gone all the way. I thought that the loss regenerated everything, that it just pissed everybody off: staff, players, everybody. So we went out and rededicated ourselves. When we hit the playoffs, we shut out two teams, we just rolled over them. We did everything right. We peaked at the right time.

Of course, we had Walter Payton that year. As a football player he was simply the best I've ever seen. I'm talking about the whole package—what you give to the game, what you take from the game, your attitude on and off the field, how you handle the media and the press, and how you play the game. He played the game with great enthusiasm and fervor, and he was exceptional. Walter was a great runner, and he was also a great blocker. He did everything—he could have played defense if we'd have put him over there, and he'd have played it pretty darn good.

I think today we have to be careful not to lose sight of football as a great sport. The game has become very big and reaches tens of millions of people each week of the season, and everybody is entitled to his piece of the game. Yet I still say that our game, the game played in the National Football League, is a very good product, and I don't think there are a lot of reasons to change everything every year. It's a good product, and we have to be careful that we don't take what is good about the product and get rid of it. This game has been played for a long time—more than eighty years—and will be played eighty more. We should not spend our time worrying about making the game shorter or speeding it up. If it's a good game, it's a good game. Think of all the great individual games we've been fortunate to watch; think of the great performances, the great plays, the great team efforts—that's NFL football.

We have to be careful not to lose sight of the game itself and the glory connected with it.

> The first stadium to have a corporate sponsor was Rich Stadium (1973) in Buffalo.

Chapter 5

photo courtesy of the Chicago Cubs

Chip Caray

Gary Pressy

John McDonough

Mary Therese Kraft

Take Me Out to the Ballgame

photo courtesy of the Chicago Cubs

A WRIGLEY FIELD MOMENT
CHIP CARAY

Chip Caray, grandson of the legendary Harry Caray and son of the longtime Atlanta Braves announcer Skip Caray, has been an announcer with the Chicago Cubs since 1998.

He was late getting here. Usually the guys sit and enjoy the game in one of the luxury boxes with our marketing staff. He was out playing golf and got stuck in the infamous Chicago traffic. The game's going on and we're not sure if and when he's going to get here. The seventh inning comes along, and there's no Ditka, so Steve (Stone) grabs the microphone and says, "Well, fans, it's the seventh-inning stretch and we've got good news and bad news. The good news is Mike Ditka was scheduled to do it.

The bad news is he's not here. So Chip and I are going to have to fill in and 'pinch-sing' for him." The crowd, of course, turns around and starts to boo us unmercifully.

Then all of a sudden Steve gets a cue from one of the marketing guys, who says, "Wait a minute, Ditka's in the house." Well, Ditka, as you know, has bad knees, bad hips, and a bad back from all those NFL days, and he's trudging up the ramps of the ballpark with that cigar sticking out of his mouth. He dashes into the booth. Just as Steve says he's here, he walks in, there is thunderous applause, he comes down, he knows he's late. He's out of breath, takes one giant gasp of air, and then of course lets out that famous rendition of "Take Me Out to the Ballgame."

He did it in his own inimitable way.

Like everybody else, I thought the way he was singing was hilarious. He knew he was late, he was rushing, he didn't want to let anybody down. I think the anticipation is always the hardest part for people who don't sing or speak in public, and Mike obviously has never been a guy who's afraid to say what's on his mind. I think he just wanted to get it over with and get it out as quickly as he could. He certainly did it in his own inimitable way. That's the way he coached the Bears. He just rode his bicycle straight through, as it were. It was great; it was wonderful.

As soon as it was over, it was almost like he had run fifty sets of forty-yard wind sprints. But he did a great job. It was certainly the most memorable rendition that we had ever heard. It was a true story: he was just stuck in traffic. We're glad he made it because it made all the highlight shows and will forever live on as one of those Wrigley Field "moments" that no one will ever forget.

photo courtesy of the Chicago Cubs

Ditka is a big baseball fan and very knowledgeable about the sport. One time he was invited to throw out the first pitch at a Cubs game. The catcher for the ceremonial first pitch was Joe Girardi. Girardi was holding a football in his right hand, but he kept it hidden behind his back. He caught Ditka's first pitch one-handed, stood up, and fired the football right at Ditka as the crowd went wild. That scene was replayed on practically every sports show in the country that evening.

Then there's the Kevin Hickey story. He pitched for the White Sox in 1983 but was released after going 1–2 with five saves. On a postgame show, after he was let go, Hickey mentioned that he needed a job. The host of the show called Mike Ditka. Hickey became a doorman at Ditka's City Lights and was in the training program when the Baltimore Orioles' general manager Roland Hemond went to eat at Ditka's, saw Hickey, and signed him for the Orioles.

photo courtesy of Gary Pressy

SINGING TOO FAST
GARY PRESSY

Gary Pressy is the organist who accompanied Ditka at Wrigley Field.

He was going to sing in the bottom of the seventh, but he ran a little late because he was playing golf and traffic was backed up. So we go into the bottom of the seventh, and Steve Stone takes the microphone and says, "The coach hasn't arrived. I guess I have to do it." Then all of a sudden here he comes. He bolts like a bat out of hell; he grabs the microphone, and in his Knute Rockne style of "Take Me Out to the Ballgame," he starts. I'm five booths down from where he is, and I'm just holding on to the key like I do with everybody. Then he starts—it looks like a polka tempo so I'm going to have to pick it up. About a quarter of the way or halfway through, I caught up with him. He went on and I just kept up with him.

The amazing part is that we scored seven runs in the bottom of the inning. We scored a touchdown—he was rallying the troops! Usually the performers come into the booth before they sing and we go over it: How are you going to sing—like a one, a two, a three? Let me hear you.

It was like a 33 rpm record going at 78 rpm.

He came late so he just came right to the booth, and I picked up his tempo. He was ahead of me, but I said, "No, no, I'm going to catch up with him." I started speeding up and I caught up to him. People didn't know what was going on. I say it was like a 33 rpm record going at 78 rpm.

Actually, I never met him that day. I did talk to him on the phone the next day. He said, "Well, I knew the organist was good. He'd keep up with anybody." Then I met him personally on Opening Day 1999, and he said, "Now listen, I'm not going to do it too fast." He did it the regular way.

Harry's the one who put Wrigley on the map with "Take Me Out to the Ballgame." I don't know who's been the best. Vince Scully was excellent; he did it like an Irish tenor. He appreciates the song and what it means to baseball. We had Kenny Rogers, the singer, not the pitcher. He did an excellent job. He came into the booth afterward and said, "I want to thank you. It's an honor." I said, "No, I want to thank you." We've had Walter Payton, Ernie Banks, Muhammad Ali. He couldn't sing, but he was there. You get to play it with all these people in different fields—Hall of Famers, singers, actors, announcers—it's great.

Ditka wasn't even the worst singer to do it. Harry was no Frank Sinatra, so if someone sang it off key, so be it. I think it turned out great when Ditka did it the first time, because it put "Take Me Out

It put "Take Me Out to the Ballgame" on the map.

to the Ballgame" on the map. After that, everybody was saying, "Now who's going to sing?"

Mike Ditka epitomizes Chicago. He was a hardworking, put-it-on-the-line type of player, and they loved that. I still see tapes of him in that game against Pittsburgh, the day after Kennedy got shot, when he ran through the whole team. He went eighty-five yards. Chicago loves that personality. And if you win, that's the icing on the cake. Since he left, the Bears have never been the same. In that one season, 1985, I can't remember a more dominant football team, and the fans loved it. He would tell the media off in no uncertain terms. He didn't care. He told the Vikings he had roller skates on in Minnesota. They loved that. That's what Chicago is.

The Tampa Bay Buccaneers have never returned a kickoff for a touchdown. In a 1998 game between the Ravens and the Vikings, three kickoffs were returned for touchdowns within seven minutes.

photo courtesy of the Chicago Cubs

SINGING AT WRIGLEY
JOHN McDONOUGH

John is the Chicago Cubs' Vice President of Marketing and Broadcasting.

I had known Mike for a while. I noticed that he was at Harry's funeral; they were close. They are kind of built out of the same cloth—two guys who have won decisive victories over life. They both play offense.

When we asked Ditka to sing, we didn't know if he could sing or not, but we're finding out that not many of them can. I think Mike's rendition has garnered more attention than anyone we've had.

We've had the biggest of the biggest of the biggest of the big, and Ditka has superceded them all.

> **I don't think anyone's ever heard a rendition as aggressive, as loud, as bombastic or enthusiastic as that one, before or since.**

Mary Therese Kraft, the young woman in our office, actually made the original contact, but when he was aware of our marketing strategy, he was flattered. He made time to do it and was very gracious about it.

There was one out in the seventh inning and he wasn't here yet. I called up to the booth and told Steve Stone and Chip Caray, our announcers, "It doesn't look like he's going to make it. You go ahead without him." Right away, there were two outs. We heard that Ditka was in the parking lot and were hoping the hitter would foul a few off—which he did. The guy stepped out of the box at the same time Ditka was running up the ramp. Well, sure enough, the guy made the third out. It was show time. "All right, ladies and gentlemen, unfortunately the coach is not with us," they said. And it was just a crescendo—a loud crescendo—of boos.

Had those fans not responded so negatively, Chip and Steve would have gone ahead. All of a sudden, almost like it was scripted out of central casting in Hollywood, Ditka appeared. He took on this persona of the coach and just let it rip. I don't think anyone's ever heard a rendition as aggressive, as loud, as bombastic or enthusiastic as that one, before or since.

The funny part about it is that with all those other obstacles—bad hips, etc.—he still made it. If you've ever been to our press box, it's the stairway to heaven. It's a long way. So it adds to the lore. We were behind in the game and after Ditka got here, he fired up the troops. It's one of the funniest pieces of video I've ever seen. It actually has won some video awards from Major League Baseball.

I didn't know whether to laugh or cry because we're trying to make this tribute to Harry somewhat dignified and honorable and respectful, yet lighthearted. Ditka's rendition took this to a brand new dimension. When you turned on the news that night, it led off every sportscast, including ESPN, FOX, and all the local news and sports shows. They played it for days and days. Then I had dinner with Mike in February of '99. We wanted to do Opening Day 1999 under the theme: "This time he's on time."

Pullman, Washington, home of Washington State University, has a population of twenty-five thousand. Martin Stadium, the home stadium for the Washington State Cougars, holds thirty-eight thousand.

photo courtesy of the Chicago Cubs

HARRY MUST BE LAUGHING IN HEAVEN
MARY THERESE KRAFT

Mary Therese Kraft is a fine young Notre Dame graduate who has the envious task of inviting singers to sing "Take Me Out the Ballgame" at Wrigley Field during the seventh-inning stretch. Singing the song is a tribute to Harry Caray and has become a popular tradition at Wrigley Field.

We invited Mike Ditka to sing "Take Me Out to the Ballgame." When he accepted we were ecstatic. The plan was for him to arrive at the ballpark directly after his golf game. The game started, and we were all running around in a panic trying to find out where he was. We called the restaurant and they said he was at the golf course. The golf course called and said, "Oh, he just left." This all happened in about the fifth inning.

We had a security person posted in the parking lot and one with me up in the booth. We just waited for him to come. As it turned out, we had to decide whether we were going to go with him or not. He arrived with two outs in the top of the seventh inning. My intern at the time, Doug Thompson, was with the security guard and they ran him up there. They radioed up to us and said Ditka had arrived. So we told our PA announcer and our message board operator, "He's here, he's in the building—we're going to go with Ditka." Then all of a sudden the third out was made. Poor Steve Stone, who's a riot, did such a great job of holding the crowd. He said, "We have an announcement: Ditka's in the building but he's not here yet, so I may have to sing by myself." The crowd started booing, not because they didn't want to hear Steve but because everyone was anticipating Mike Ditka.

In the meantime, our security guard was running this poor guy— who has had two hip surgeries and a heart attack—up our back stairway, which has about three flights of stairs and four ramps. We got him up to the top of the stairway, and Steve Stone said, "The coach has arrived." Everybody in the crowd just went crazy. We told him we were going to prep him on the way up and that we'd been waiting for him. We meant that we were not going to sing without him. But I think he thought we meant that we weren't going to start the

> Only two teams in the last quarter century
> have won college football's national title with
> a freshman quarterback: Miami in 1983
> with Bernie Kosar and Oklahoma in
> 1985 with Jamelle Holieway.

game until he sang. So he just belted it out like no other. Oh, it was so funny, and his expression after was just the most comical thing we saw all year.

Everyone's faces were in a state of confusion. They started to sing with him, but just couldn't keep up. Everyone started with "Take me out to the ballgame," but they just lost him after that. This had never happened; the seventh inning stretch was not sung. Everyone was just in awe. Our organist Gary Pressy kept right up with him. He followed him to a T, which is amazing. It was unreal. As soon as he finished, everyone was like, "What just happened?" The bleacher section did a chorus of their own and sang the whole song over again because it was just too fast.

We got him up to the top of the stairway, and Steve Stone said, "The coach has arrived." Everybody in the crowd just went crazy.

My heart has never beaten so fast. It went from a total state of panic—"I have no idea where he is"—to "Okay, he's here, let's run him up." Then we just took a huge breath, and it didn't hit anybody until that night when it was aired across the country on ESPN and CNN. Diana, his wife, called and asked for a copy of it, because she hadn't seen it. People were just calling like crazy. They were laughing and saying it was the best rendition. When you look at it, you know Harry has to be laughing hysterically in heaven because it was so Harry-esque and so Ditka-esque. The way he said, "One, two, three strikes you're out"—it was a riot.

He could not have been nicer. He stayed on the air with Chip and Steve; they couldn't even cut to a commercial because it was so late. He was wonderful. He interviewed with the press and was so apologetic. He said, "I'm so sorry; I didn't realize it would take so long to get here from the golf course. I got stuck on Addison." We ask everybody who sings to autograph the score and some baseballs to auction off at the end of the season. He said, "Oh, I'll sign anything you want. I feel terrible." I asked if he would mind going on WGN radio, and he said, "Oh, I'll do anything, I feel so bad." He was funny.

I had never met him before in person, and he was great. He took pictures with everybody, signed anything anybody wanted him to sign, and did a great interview with the media. He was wonderful, and I think he really loved it. He won an award for us, which really put this entire "seventh-inning stretch" song on the map. From that point on, we had people calling us up to offer to sing because of the exposure he was able to get for us.

Ditka sang on Opening Day 1999, and I have to say that he still can't carry a tune. Our theme this year was: "This time he's on time." This time he sang much slower. I think it was important to him to come back and do it again and do it right. He's not a strong singer, but he's a phenomenal guy all around. When we approached him this year, we told him about the award that MLB had presented to us because of his performance; I think he was kind of in awe. Major League Baseball gave us the award for "Blooper of the Year." It probably isn't something to be too proud of, but it was pretty funny.

Ditka is such an amazing icon; it's really impressive. You see that stern face, that rugged blue-collar persona on TV, the Ditka that

> When Mack Brown became the head coach at the University of Texas, he became the second-highest-paid college football coach ever, yet he had never even won a conference title.

When you look at it, you know Harry has to be laughing hysterically in heaven because it was so Harry-esque and so Ditka-esque.

broke his arm in the locker room when he was so mad—this rough, tough guy. The first time I met him, I was almost taken aback. His face is such a caricature. Here is a man who is no longer affiliated with Chicago—he coaches an opposing team now and just has a restaurant in Chicago—but is loved more than any other Chicagoan right now, and that is really impressive. The fans still love the coach and think of him as Chicago's.

We had a hard time, because usually we play music, make an announcement, and lead up to who's going to sing. Of course, we didn't want to play anything Saints-related, and we almost didn't want to play anything Bears-related, since he's not head coach anymore. So we just played "Chicago," because that's what he is. He is Chicago. My generation, especially, admires him. He's got that Midwest mentality that everybody appreciates and associates with. It's that rugged image of someone who worked hard all his life, has definite morals and ethics, or at least is someone you can respect. Who doesn't really appreciate and support that?

More NFL games have been played at Wrigley Field than at any other stadium in the country. Mile High Stadium in Denver is in second place.

MIKE DITKA ON HARRY CARAY

photo courtesy of *Dallas Cowboys Weekly*

It's hard to describe Harry without getting into a long description. He really enjoyed life. He was fun to be around. And he was real. He was genuine. There was no phoniness to Harry Caray. I loved him for that. He didn't make it a secret that when he wanted a beer, he had a beer. There was no put-on, no front. He was just real people.

He took time with people. That's the thing I noticed. Every time I was with him, he always took time with people. He always signed the autographs. He talked to the people. A lot of it could have been very aggravating, but he did it. A lot of celebrities won't do that, and I thought that was one of the greatest things about him.

Ditka's famed restaurant on Chicago's West Ontario Street pre-dated Harry Caray's eatery as a trendy place. But Caray's had the staying power. Ditka now is associated with another restaurant a few blocks further east, in the Streeterville area. Caray did patronize the original Ditka's.

Harry was at Ditka's City Lights a few times. Actually, the guy who put Harry in business with his restaurant, Ben Stein, was a partner in our business for a while.

Harry and I shot a commercial up at the bar at Ditka's (Restaurant) by the (O'Hare) airport. It was funnier than heck, because it was not very hard to do, but Harry had had a few pops and he was continuing to drink his Budweiser as we were trying to do the shoot. Oh my gosh. It took him about twenty-five to thirty shoots to get it. After a while, I was the problem because I was laughing so hard at him. But he was beautiful.

He loved the Cubs. He had a strong relationship with the Cardinals and he worked for the White Sox. But I don't think any relationship was as strong as his with the Cubs. I think he probably agonized more over that relationship than over any of the others. He really just wanted them to win.

Even I'm pulling for the Cubs now. Believe me.

> Alabama has the most college football bowl wins with twenty-eight and the most losses with twenty. Southern Cal is second with twenty-five and thirteen.

BIBLIOGRAPHY

Anderson, Terry. *The Movement and the Sixties*. New York: Oxford University Press, 1995.

Bahas, Dr. Gabriel. *Keep off the Grass*. Pleasantville, N.Y.: Readers Digest Press, 1976.

Bayless, Skip. *The Boys: Jones vs. Johnson and the Feud that Rocked America's Team*. New York: Pocket Books, 1994.

Bayless, Skip. *God's Coach*. New York: Simon & Schuster, 1990.

Blair, Sam. *Dallas Cowboys: Pro or Con?* New York: Doubleday, 1970.

Dent, Jim. *King of the Cowboys: The Life and Times of Jerry Jones*. Holbrook, Mass.: Adams Publishing, 1995.

Dorsett, Tony, with Harvey Frommer. *Running Tough*. New York: Doubleday, 1989.

Garrison, Walt, and John Tullius. *Once a Cowboy*. New York: Random House, 1988.

Gent, Pete. *North Dallas Forty*. New York: William Morrow, 1973.

Goodman, Michael E. *Chicago Bears* (NFL Today). Mankato, Minn.: Creative Education, 1996.

Harris, David. *The League: The Rise and Decline of the NFL*. New York: Bantam Books, 1986.

Henderson, Thomas "Hollywood," and Peter Knobler. *Out of Control: Confessions of an NFL Casualty*. New York: G. P. Putnam & Sons, 1987.

Johnson, Jimmy, as told to Ed Hinton. *Turning the Thing Around*. New York: Hyperion, 1993.

Keteyian, Armen. *Ditka: Monster of the Midway*. New York: Pocket Books, 1992.

Kowat, Don. *The Rich Who Own Sports*. New York: Random House, 1977.

Lamb, Kevin. *Portrait of Victory: Chicago Bears 1985*. Provo, Utah: Final Four Publications, 1986.

Landry, Tom, with Gregg Lewis. *Tom Landry: An Autobiography*. New York: Zondervan Publishing, 1990.

Leslie, Warren. *Dallas City Limit*. New York: Grossman Publishers, 1964.

Mausser, Wayne. *Chicago Bears Facts and Trivia* (Sports Facts and Trivia). South Bend, Ind.: E. B. Houchin Company, 1997.

Nolen, Claude H. *The Negro's Image in the South: The Anatomy of White Supremacy*. Louisville: University of Kentucky Press, 1967.

O'Connor, Richard. *The Oil Barons: Men of Greed and Grandeur*. Boston: Little, Brown, 1971.

Payne, Darwin. *Big D: Triumphs and Troubles of an American Supercity in The 20th Century*. Dallas: Three Forks Press, 1994.

Priestly, James. *A Saga of Wealth*. New York: G. P. Putnam & Sons, 1978.

Rentzel, Lance. *When All the Laughter Died in Sorrow*. New York: Saturday Review Press, 1972.

Rothaus, James R. *The Chicago Bears*. Mankato, Minn.: Creative Education, 1981.

St. John, Bob. *The Landry Legend*. Dallas: Word Books, 1989.

St. John, Bob. *Landry: The Man Inside*. Dallas: Word Books, 1979.

St. John, Bob. *Tex!: The Man Who Built the Cowboys*. New York: Prentice Hall, 1988.

Schapp, Dick. *Quarterbacks Have All the Fun*. Chicago: Playboy Press, 1974.

Singletary, Mike, and Armen Keteyian. *Calling the Shots: Inside the Chicago Bears*. Chicago: Contemporary Books, 1986.

Smith, Emmitt, with Steve Delsohn. *The Emmitt Zone*. New York: Crown, 1994.

Stamborski. Jim. *Don't Get Me Wrong: Mike Ditka's Insights, Outbursts, Kudos, and Comebacks*. Chicago: Chicago Review Press, 1988.

Staubach, Roger, with Frank Luksa. *Time Enough to Win*. Waco, Tex.: Word Incorporated, 1980.

Stowers, Carlton. *Journey to Triumph*. Dallas: Taylor Publishing, 1982.

Switzer, Barry, with Bud Shrake. *Bootlegger's Boy*. New York: William Morrow, 1990.

Thomas, Duane, and Paul Zimmerman. *Duane Thomas and the Fall of America's Team*. New York: Warner Books, 1988.

Toomay, Pat. *The Crunch*. New York: W. W. Norton, 1975.

Vass, George. *George Halas and the Chicago Bears*. Chicago: Regnery, 1971.

Whittingham, Richard. *Bears: In Their Own Words: Chicago Bear Greats Talk About the Team, the Game, the Coaches, and the Times of Their Lives*. Chicago: Contemporary Books, 1992.

Whittingham, Richard. *The Chicago Bears: An Illustrated History*. Chicago: Rand McNally, 1979.

Whittingham, Richard. *The Chicago Bears: From George Halas to Super Bowl XX, an Illustrated History*. New York: Simon and Schuster, 1986.

Wiley, Ralph. *Why Black People Tend to Shout*. New York: Birch Lane Press, 1991.

Wismer, Harry. *The Public Calls It Sport*. New York: Prentice Hall, 1965.

Wolfe, Jane. *The Murchisons: The Rise and Fall of a Texas Dynasty*. New York: St. Martin's Press, 1989.

About Rich...

Rich Wolfe was raised near Lost Nation, Iowa, played basketball and baseball at Notre Dame, and has lived in Scottsdale, Arizona, since 1975. He is a sports marketing consultant, has owned a minor league basketball team, and currently owns a Central Hockey League franchise. His previous books are *Sports Fans Who Made Headlines* and *I Remember Harry Caray.*

Publisher's Note

An editor's nightmare . . . One day out of nowhere, a jumbled pile of fifty incomplete transcriptions with no corresponding photographs gets dumped on your desk along with marching orders to turn them into a coherent, complete book in less than three weeks. You have a crazed author and a demanding, knows-enough-to-be-dangerous publisher to contend with, as well as a few other projects on your plate.

What do you do? What would Mike Ditka do?

You grit your teeth, clench your fists—and make it happen. And that's just what the editorial department at Triumph Books did.

And then there's Rich Wolfe, a one-man wrecking crew, who came up with the concept and burned up the phone lines to get the raw material for this book. Rich exploded onto the scene at our offices eight weeks prior to his demanded project completion date with guns blazing, holding an oversized plastic garbage bag filled with soggy papers, transcription tapes, and his signature case of Diet Coke™. Go get 'em, Rich!

Also, to the publisher of Mike Ditka's autobiography, Aaron Cohodes: it was a heck of a ride—a blessing and a curse rolled into one (though still trying to get a handle on the blessing part).